Essential Algarve

by Christopher Catling

Christopher Catling has written more than 30 travel guides. He is a regular contributor to travel magazines on the Internet and in print. His books on London, Florence, Venice and Amsterdam are inspired by a keen interest in art and architecture, while his love of the countryside is reflected in guides to Madeira, Umbria and Crete.

Above: *the beach at Carvoeiro*

AA Publishing

Above: *typical* azulejo

Find out more about AA Publishing and the wide range of services the AA provides by visiting our website at www.theAA.com

Written by Christopher Catling
Revised (2002) by Lindsay Bennett
Original photography by Michelle Chaplow

First Published 1999. Reprinted Jun 1999, Feb 2000. Reprinted 2001, verified and updated. Reprinted May 2001, Feb 2002.
Second edition 2002

Published by AA Publishing, a trading name of Automobile Association Developments Limited, whose registered office is Millstream, Maidenhead Road, Windsor, Berkshire SL4 5GD. Registered number 1878835.

A CIP catalogue record for this book is available from the British Library.

ISBN 0 7495 3466 4

The contents of this publication are believed correct at the time of printing. Nevertheless, the publishers cannot be held responsible for any errors or omissions or for changes in the details given in this guide or for the consequences of any reliance on the information provided by the same. Assessments of attractions, hotels, restaurants and so forth are based upon the author's own experience and, therefore, descriptions given in this guide necessarily contain an element of subjective opinion which may not reflect the publisher's opinion or dictate a reader's own experience on another occasion.

We have tried to ensure accuracy in this guide, but things do change and we would be grateful if readers would advise us of any inaccuracies they may encounter.

Colour separation: Pace Colour, Southampton

Printed and bound in Italy by Printer Trento Srl

Contents

About this Book

KEY TO SYMBOLS

- map reference to the maps found in the What to See section (see below)
- address or location
- telephone number
- opening times
- restaurant or café on premises or near by
- nearest underground train station
- nearest bus/tram route
- nearest overground train station
- ferry crossings and boat excursions
- travel by air
- tourist information
- facilities for visitors with disabilities
- admission charge
- other places of interest near by
- other practical information
- ➤ indicates the page where you will find a fuller description

Essential *Algarve* is divided into five sections to cover the most important aspects of your visit to the Algarve.

Viewing the Algarve pages 5–14
An introduction to the Algarve by the author.
The Algarve's Features
Essence of the Algarve
The Shaping of the Algarve
Peace and Quiet
The Algarve's Famous

Top Ten pages 15–26
The author's choice of the Top Ten places to see in the Algarve, listed in alphabetical order, each with practical information.

What to See pages 27–90
The four main areas of the Algarve, each with its own brief introduction and an alphabetical listing of the main attractions.
Practical information
Snippets of 'Did you know…' information
5 suggested walks
4 suggested tours
2 features

Where To… pages 91–116
Detailed listings of the best places to eat, stay, shop, take the children and be entertained.

Practical Matters pages 117–124
A highly visual section containing essential travel information.

Maps
All map references are to the individual maps found in the What to See section of this guide.

For example, the village of Estói has the reference 29E2 – indicating the page on which the map is located and the grid square in which the village is to be found. A list of the maps that have been used in this travel guide can be found in the index.

Prices
Where appropriate, an indication of the cost of an establishment is given by **£** signs: **£££** denotes higher prices, **££** denotes average prices, while **£** denotes lower charges.

Star Ratings
Most of the places described in this book have been given a separate rating:

Do not miss
Highly recommended
Worth seeing

Viewing the Algarve

Above: *watching and waiting*
Right: *bringing home the catch*

Christopher Catling's Algarve

Traditional boats are still used to fish for tuna, cod and sardines

When I first visited the Algarve in the 1970s, Portugal was only just opening its doors to the world, having finally shrugged off a dictatorship that had clung on to power since 1932. Keen to catch up with the rest of Europe, Portugal leapt in a decade from the Middle Ages to the post-industrial age, and the freedoms that came in the wake of the revolution resulted in the Algarve's rapid development.

More than a quarter of a century on, the Algarve is firmly on the map as a rewarding and inexpensive holiday destination. Fortunately, it has managed to achieve this without overwhelming the features that make it so special. Swathes of the Algarve remain delightfully wild and unexploited, with scores of little bays and coves where you can laze the day away if you choose, while the endless expanses of golden sand farther east allow everyone to stake out their own private beach territory.

Perhaps the most attractive feature of the Algarve is simply that it combines so many different attractions – beaches, luxurious hotels and manicured golf courses, nightlife and sunshine. Equally, the Algarve satisfies my taste for exploring churches, slipping into centuries-old hilltowns to observe the way of life, or rambling gently along cliff paths and through orange-scented groves, enjoying the wild flowers and butterflies.

Integration

The Algarvian readiness to embrace all comers is part of a tradition of tolerance dating back many centuries. Many of the Jews expelled from Spain in 1492 by the Catholic monarchs Ferdinand and Isabella found a new home in the Algarve, and the region's architecture, cooking, ceramics and agriculture all result from the absorption of North African and Spanish settlers and their cultural influences.

The Algarve's Features

Geography

• The Algarve, Portugal's southernmost province, is separated from the Alentejo, the next province north, by a range of low mountains known as the Serra de Monchique to the west and the Serra do Caldeirão to the east.

• To the west and south the region is bounded by the Atlantic Ocean, and to the east the River Guadiana forms the frontier between Portugal and Andalucia (Spain).

• The Algarve represents about one-twentieth of Portugal's total area (4,960sq km) and measures about 135km east to west and between 27 and 50km north to south.

Landscape

• Topographically, the Algarve divides into three main regions: the coast (*litoral*), where most of the intensive tourist development is located; the foothills (*barrocal*), where most of the agriculture is concentrated; and the almost uninhabited mountains (*serra*), which support extensive cork oak forests.

• The Algarve includes mainland Europe's southwesternmost point, the legendary Cabo de São Vicente (Cape St Vincent). The western end of the coast is composed of eroded sandstone cliffs of many colourful hues, with numerous marine grottoes and wind-eroded rock stacks, while towards the east the coast is flat and sandy, with long beaches and barrier islands forming shallow lagoons.

Climate

• The mountains separating the Algarve from the Alentejo also shelter it from cold continental air in winter, so that the region's winter climate is markedly milder than the rest of Portugal, though it does have high rainfall, due to Atlantic fronts.

• The coast is traditionally divided into the *barlavento* (windward) region (from Cape St Vincent to Albufeira), which bears the brunt of the southwesterly winds, and the more sheltered *sotavento* (leeward).

Exports

Portugal is the world's biggest producer of cork, and much of it is grown in the Algarve and the Alentejo. Traditional almond and fig production, while still important, is in decline, but citrus production is increasing and large areas of the foothills are covered in orange and lemon groves. Tuna, cod and sardine fishing and canning are important, but the industry has not modernised and faces strong competition from Spanish fishermen with more modern fleets.

Natural sculptures formed from the rock at Algar Seco

Essence of the Algarve

Landscape and climate combine in the Algarve to create a region of year-round appeal. In winter the Algarve basks in balmy sunshine. In summer it remains green and equable due to the cooling effect of Atlantic breezes. Travelling around, you will encounter breathtaking views: sheer cliffs battered by Atlantic waves at Cabo de São Vicente (Cape St Vincent); sheltered valleys with their patchwork of orange groves; vineyards and olive trees or castle-topped peaks, with Moorish-style houses tumbling down the hillside; and brightly painted sardine boats in the harbours.

Nothing beats the taste of fresh sardines grilled on a wood fire

THE 10 ESSENTIALS

If you only have a short time to visit the Algarve, or would like to get a complete picture of the region, here are the essentials:

- **Blow the cobwebs away** on top of the cliffs at Fim do Mundo (World's End, ➤ 18), as Cape St Vincent is known, gazing out over the waves to the distant horizon.
- **Step back in time** on a visit to Silves (➤ 44), which under Moorish rule boasted marble-clad palaces and bazaars full of eastern splendour.
- **Go for dinner** in a traditional restaurant and listen to the plaintive sound of Portuguese *fado* music (➤ 112).
- **Eat lunch in Portimão** (➤ 52), where fresh sardines are unloaded from fishing boats and cooked at rough-and-ready harbourside stalls, advertising their presence with the delicious scent of charcoal-grilled fish.
- **Walk to the Fonte de Benémola** (➤ 73) for a taste of the Algarvian countryside, as a contrast to the more developed coast.
- **Visit Praia da Rocha** (➤ 53) at sunset to enjoy the changing colours of the sandstone rocks and cliffs as the sun goes down.
- **Play a round of golf** at one of the region's 24 golf courses (➤ 115). The Algarve is one of Europe's top golfing-holiday destinations.
- **Join in a village festivity** (➤ 116) for the fun of noisy fireworks and to taste local wines and kebabs or fish cooked over an open wood fire.
- **Spend a lazy day** on the beach but, rather than joining the hordes at Albufeira or Monte Gordo, head for one of the barrier islands, such as the Ilha da Tavira (➤ 79), and find your own private area of sand dunes and sea.
- **Visit the capital,** Faro (➤ 62), for its sophistication, its timeless Old Town, the ethnographic museum illustrating a way of life that only just survives, and to enjoy the *frisson* of the skull-lined Capela dos Ossos in the Carmo church.

Orange groves scent the air with heady blossom and fruit

Watching the waves beat against the Algarvian shore

The Shaping of the Algarve

2000 BC
Bronze Age people migrate to the region from North Africa and establish settlements at Lagos, Tavira and Lagoa.

1000 BC
Phoenician traders from the eastern Mediterranean establish trading posts along the Algarve coast, exporting salt-preserved sardines and tuna.

The caravel was a mainstay of Portuguese exploration

550 BC
The Carthaginians, from modern-day Tunisia, found the town of Portimão, known in the 3rd century BC as Portus Hanibalis, after the great Carthaginian general.

197 BC
The Romans invade the Iberian Peninsula and settle the Algarve. Resistance to the Romans leads to years of guerilla warfare until Caesar finally quells the region in his campaigns of 61–45 BC.

5th century AD
Christianised Visigoths migrate into the Algarve from the north and settle in the region, establishing the first cathedral at Faro.

AD 711
Arabs invade the Algarve from Ceuta in Northern Africa and conquer the region over three years.

AD 712
Moorish leader Muce-Ben-Noçair adopts Silves as the regional capital. The Moors name their new territory Al-Gharb, the 'land of the west', from which the modern name for the region – Algarve – is derived.

1189
The Christian reconquest of the Iberian Peninsula achieves a notable victory at Silves, when the besieged city surrenders to an army led by King Sancho I, which is augmented by Christian Crusaders from northern Europe.

1191
The Moors recapture the city and continue to rule in the Algarve, long after they are driven out of Lisbon and the north of Portugal.

1249
Sancho's successors, Afonso II and III, continue the struggle against the Moors, taking Tavira in 1239, then Faro, and finally Silves. The Moors finally leave the region, which becomes part of the Kingdom of Portugal.

1443
Prince Henry the Navigator sets up his court at Sagres and establishes a school of navigation, ship-building and astronomy. As the sponsor of many expeditions to explore the West African coast and the islands of the Madeiran archipelago, he lays the foundation for Portugal's subsequent pre-eminence as a maritime trading nation.

1444
One of Europe's first slave markets is established at Lagos, following western exploration of what is now the Senegal estuary.

1485
Portugal becomes a major commercial power,

Philip II of Spain conquered Portugal in 1580

with trading posts in western and southern Africa, Asia, Indonesia and Brazil, but Lisbon takes over from the Algarvian ports as the departure point for voyages of discovery, and the Algarve becomes a relative backwater.

1580
The Algarve comes under Spanish rule after Philip II conquers Portugal.

1640
Border towns on the Guadiana River bear the brunt of the fighting as the Portuguese revolt against Spanish rule and regain their independence under King João IV.

1755
A series of earthquakes destroys many towns in the Algarve, and the subsequent tidal waves block river estuaries and ports with sand. The Marquês de Pombal, King José I's chief minister, rebuilds the region's towns.

1807
Napoleon invades Portugal and the royal family flees to Brazil. The Algarve puts up fierce resistance to the French, and a group of fishermen from Olhão later sail to Rio de Janeiro in a tiny boat to tell their exiled king of Napoleon's defeat.

1889
The Faro to Lisbon railway is opened.

1932
President Salazar establishes a military dictatorship in Portugal. Portugal remains neutral during World War II, but severs relations with Nazi Germany.

1974
The Carnation Revolution: Portugal becomes a democracy after soldiers overthrow the post-war dictatorship. Flowers in the barrels of their guns are a symbol of peace.

1986
Portugal becomes a member of the EU, releasing development funds for the improvement of the region's infrastructure, including the main east–west motorway and the bridge linking Portugal and Spain across the Guadiana River.

1996
After years of drought that have left the region's reservoirs dry, the Algarve experiences record rainfall.

2002
The Portuguese say goodbye to the *escudo,* as euro banknotes and coins are introduced, replacing their old national currency.

Salazar's dictatorial regime ended with a peaceful revolution

Peace and Quiet

Almonds, introduced by the Moors, bloom like snow in spring

Away from it All

The Algarve is at its most developed south of the IP1 motorway between Faro and Albufeira. Simply to drive away from this area is to escape quickly and easily from the bustle of modern life and discover the many faces of the Algarve. South of Faro is the extensive Reserva Natural da Ria Formosa (➤ 26), a series of salt-water lagoons and salt pans separated from the open sea by scores of sandy islands, some tiny, others stretching for several kilometres. The warm lagoon water supports many types of marine life. This in turn attracts flocks of wading birds, from shy flamingos to the storks that flap lazily over the roof-tops, building their nests on church towers, telegraph poles and ancient olive trees.

Further west, the marsh systems and river estuaries around Portimão, Lagos and Burgau are full of birds. You do not have to be a knowledgeable ornithologist to spot the ubiquitous flocks of cattle egrets, with their hunched shoulders, long probing beaks and pure white feathers, or to enjoy the hunting skill of the kestrels and sparrowhawks that skim the fields in search of prey.

Bird Migration

The Algarve is also an important staging post for migrating birds, which pass down through the Iberian Peninsula in October before making the final leg of their journey to Africa. Returning the same way in March and April, they ride the southwesterly winds from Africa, exploiting the fact that spring and summer come early here in order to feed on the insects that are already thick in the air before heading for nesting sites in northern Europe. Cape St Vincent, Europe's southwesterly tip, is the place to see birds streaming past the cliffs or using the updraughts to carry them inland – these range from large seabirds, such as gannets, skuas, petrels and shearwaters, to swallows, swifts, warblers and colourful bee-eaters.

Inland Algarve

The hilly Algarvian interior is covered in a network of paths and mule tracks, which are perfect for exploring on foot. Large-scale walking maps are difficult to come by and generally out of date, but the Algarve Tourist Authority publishes a *Guide to Walks*, containing 20 short routes, and more ambitious walks are detailed in the excellent *Landscapes of Portugal*, by Brian and Eileen Anderson (Sunflower Guides).

Walkers head for the Algarve any time from late October onwards, but the best time to come is March to

Algarvian Trees

The carob tree is widely grown in the Algarve because its long, bean-like seeds are used as cattle fodder. You will often see it growing in groves, partnered by gnarled old olives and fig trees. Mimosas are commonly planted along road verges, their puffy yellow flowers scattering a delicious almond-like scent during the spring.

May, when the countryside is a mass of flowers and butterflies. A short walk in the hills will take you from orange groves, heady with the cloying scent of citrus blossom, to bare slopes dense with sticky-leaved cistus (rock rose), bearing big white flowers. Rarer flowers bloom in the undergrowth, including many kinds of orchid, as well as numerous bulbs, such as the petticoat-hoop narcissus. Every wayside is bright with the searing yellow of the Bermuda buttercup, which colonises every inch of uncultivated space, and the sound of cicadas in the undergrowth can reach a deafening pitch.

Walking
The Algarve Walkers Club is a group of English expatriates living in the Algarve who meet for weekly rambles.
☎ 282 449098 for further information.

Walkers set off towards the atalaia *(obelisk) at Luz*

The Algarve's Famous

Henry the Navigator founded Portugal's global empire

Henry the Navigator

Prince Henry the Navigator (Dom Henrique O Navegador, 1394–1460) was the third son of João I of Portugal. Though he only ever made one sea journey, he nevertheless single-handedly set Portugal on the course that was to make her one of the great maritime powers of Europe. He did this by setting up a college at Sagres, symbolically choosing a point that looks out from the tip of Europe to what was then the vast unknown of the Atlantic. Gathering around him the best astronomers, naval engineers and navigators of his day, he funded their research and their voyages of discovery. The invention of the caravel, a small, light but extremely buoyant and manoeuvrable ship, eventually enabled explorers and merchants to reach India, the Far East and the Americas.

Gil Eanes

Theorising about the possibility of land beyond the horizon is one thing, but sailing into the unknown is a different matter, and Gil Eanes (*c*1400–88), a native of Lagos, was the brave navigator who took up the challenge. Sailing round the coast of West Africa in 1434, he led modern Europe's first-ever expedition around Cape Bojador, popularly believed to mark the end of the world, with only boiling monster-ridden seas beyond. Proving otherwise, Eanes mapped the coastal waters and encouraged others to follow in his wake.

Bartolomeu Dias

In 1487, Bartolomeu Dias (*c*1450–1500) set out from Portimão at the head of the first expedition since ancient Roman times to round the tip of southern Africa. The storm-battered tip, which he named Cape Torment because of its extraordinarily unpredictable currents, was more optimistically renamed the Cape of Good Hope on the instructions of King João II, who saw it as the route to the riches of the East. The Cape was to prove Dias' nemesis, for he died when his ship was wrecked sailing round it in 1500.

The Moorish Legacy

Though the former great names of the Algarve remain unsung in the West, Arab historians list a number of Algarvian scientists, poets, philosophers and astronomers, and it was due to contact between Moorish and European traders that Arabic numbers began to be used in the West, replacing the cumbersome Roman system. These learned scholars also introduced many innovations in the fields of arithmetic, astronomy, navigation, medicine, agriculture, law and ceramics.

Top Ten

Above: *the Moorish castle at Silves*
Right: *traditional festive costume*

1
Algar Seco (Carvoeiro)

28C2

About 1km east of Carvoeiro, signposted to the left from the centre of town

Small café (£) among the rocks; several others in Carvoeiro

Free

Carvoeiro (➤ 47)

Pitted pillars, grottoes and crystal-clear seas await you at Algar Seco

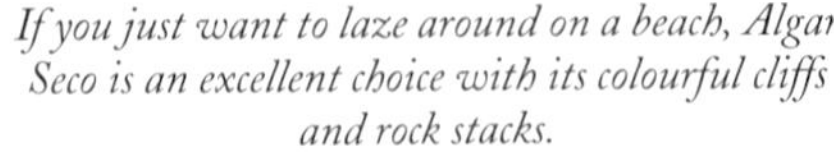

If you just want to laze around on a beach, Algar Seco is an excellent choice with its colourful cliffs and rock stacks.

There is a marked difference between the beaches of the sandy eastern *sotavento* (leeward) section of the Algarve and the rocky western, or *barlavento* (windward) section. Armação de Pêra, to the west of Albufeira, is the axis on which the Algarve is tilted and the point at which this decisive change takes place. West of here the land rises gradually until it reaches the high cliffs and boiling seas of Cape St Vincent; to the east, flatter coastal terrain gives way to endless strands of golden sand, gently dipping into a warm and shallow sea.

The cause of the tilt is the collision zone between the Eurasian and African continental plates, which lies only a short way south of the Algarvian coast. The African plate is moving northwestwards, pushing the European land mass slowly upwards. This explains why the junction between land and sea is more dramatic in the west, marked by steep sandstone cliffs, and why the coast is broken up into a series of rock-strewn coves.

The result is a series of wind-and-sea eroded rocks whose evocative shapes make this part of the coast unique, and nowhere else has these rock formations in such quantity or variety as Algar Seco. Here, children will love exploring the rock platforms and pillars, the arches, chambers and caves, the miniature gorges, clefts and pools that litter the shore. Snorkellers will find weed-encrusted rocks like miniature coral reefs below the waves. There is not much sand, but the other features compensate, including the colourful show of light and shade that begins as the sun sinks at dusk.

2
Alte

Discover the many charms of this pretty hill village, built around a series of gushing springs (fontes).

Alte sits on top of a hill in the limestone foothills known as the Barrocal (➤ 67). Winding roads climb to the village through a region dubbed the 'Garden of the Algarve', where fig trees and citrus groves surrounded by drystone walls alternate with almond orchards and stands of gnarled and ancient olive trees.

Brazilian gold provides the finery in this baroque church

The focal point of the village is the parish church, one of the most interesting in the Algarve because of its wealth of 18th-century woodwork and its baroque *azulejos*. Rope mouldings (in the Manueline style) decorate the west door, the vaulting of the chancel and the arch of the so-called 'Chapel of the Landowner', with its coat of arms of the counts of Alte. Painted and gilded woodwork surrounds the altar, while angelic musicians and cherubs scamper among the vine and acanthus leaves.

From the church, cobbled lanes lead eastwards for a five-minute stroll to a series of springs (*fontes*), where the water gushes out of pipes set in niches decorated with *azulejos* and plaques inscribed with verses by the local poet, Cândido Guerreiro (1871–1953), in praise of water. The water here betrays its volcanic origins with a sulphur smell, but it tastes fresh enough and many local people come here to fill huge containers, believing that the water prolongs their life and keeps them healthy.

About 200m upstream is another set of springs, Fonte Grande. From here, keen walkers can follow the footpath upstream for 3km to the source of the River Alte in the foot of the Serra do Caldeirão mountain range. Less keen hikers can rest at one of the two restaurants, or picnic at tables under the shade of the trees, before browsing through the crafts on sale in the *artesanato* shops around the church square.

29D2

20km north of Albufeira

Church: daily 8–1, 3–7

Fonte Pequeña bar/restaurant (££)
☎ 289 478509

Free

Loulé (➤ 68), Silves (➤ 44)

3
Cabo de São Vicente

28A2

6km west of Sagres

Snack bars on site and cafés (£) in Sagres; Fortaleza de Beliche restaurant (£££) on the road from Sagres to the Cape

None

Free

Sagres (► 37)

Come at sunset on a clear day to get the most from a visit to the cliffs that were once believed to mark the end of the world.

Cabo de São Vicente is the most southwesterly point of the European mainland (not counting Madeira, the Canary Islands and the Azores). It really looks and feels like the end of the earth (which is why the Portuguese dubbed it 'Fim do Mundo' centuries ago). With its towering cliffs plunging 70m to the pounding surf, and its stiff westerly breezes, this is a place that stirs the imagination and works a strong magic over the many visitors who flock here.

The Romans, recognising the spiritual pull of the spot, built a temple to the presiding *numen* (deity). Nothing now remains of this, but there is a lighthouse whose beam can be seen up to 100km out to sea. The lighthouse is open to visitors if the keeper is not otherwise engaged. If you do get to look inside, you will see Europe's biggest lighthouse lantern, lit by a massive 3,000-watt bulb.

Your own memories and impressions will be dictated by the weather: stallholders selling chunky handknitted sweaters in the car park are a reminder that it can be chilly here no matter how hot it is a few miles inland, and there can be fog, rain or howling gales. On the other hand, nothing enhances the pristine beauty of Cabo de São Vicente more than watching sea birds playing in the air above the crashing waves, or the sight of the rose-tinted sun sinking slowly into the ocean at dusk.

Beyond lies only the ocean – the view from Cabo de São Vicente

4
Caldas de Monchique

Visit this centuries-old spa town in the Monchique hills and sample the sulphurous waters once enjoyed by the Romans.

28B2

20km north of Portimão

Termas de Monchique (£££) 282 910910

Bus service links Caldas de Monchique to Portimão

None

Free

For more information: www.monchiquetermas.com is the spa website

Built for indulgence – the spas and casino of Caldas de Monchique

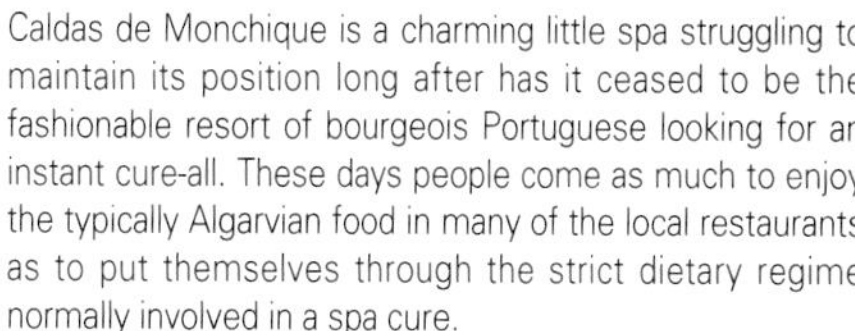

Caldas de Monchique is a charming little spa struggling to maintain its position long after has it ceased to be the fashionable resort of bourgeois Portuguese looking for an instant cure-all. These days people come as much to enjoy the typically Algarvian food in many of the local restaurants as to put themselves through the strict dietary regime normally involved in a spa cure.

As with many spas built at the crux of the 19th and 20th centuries, the buildings reflect the belief that good company and relaxation are just as important for the cure as water consumption – hence a casino was regarded as *de rigueur* and the hotels were built with grand public rooms for dancing and conversation. The spa complex has benefited greatly from a recent renovation project and was reopened with great aplomb by the Portuguese Minister of Tourism in the summer of 2001.

The Romans got here first. More than 2,000 years ago they built a spa on the site of the present sanatorium, calling it Mons Cicus, from which the spa, and the nearby market town of Monchique, derive their name. Today it is the picturesque appearance of the little spa that appeals, set amongst dense woodland on the edge of a mini ravine, with its pastel-painted houses in fanciful styles.

Footpaths thread through woods and along the river, taking you to springs where you can sample the water – pleasant enough to taste even if it is warm and smells sulphurous. For something stronger, there are cafés where you can sip coffee, or try the local speciality *medronho,* a fiery liqueur distilled from fermented arbutus berries.

5
Capela dos Ossos (Faro)

Intimations of mortality may occupy your mind as you contemplate the skull-encrusted Chapel of the Bones.

Skulls and bones are arranged as if in a decorative frieze

 63B3

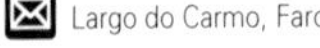 Largo do Carmo, Faro

 Oct–Apr Mon–Fri 10–1, 3–5, Sat 10–1; May–Sep Mon–Fri 10–1, 3–6, Sat 10–1

Cafés in the pedestrianised streets at the centre of Faro, such as Avenida D Francisco Gomes

Few

 Inexpensive

Historic centre and museums of Faro (► 62–65)

The Chapel of the Bones is a must for unsqueamish children, who will find this ghoulish site enormous fun.

Unfortunately, the Carmelite monks who created the chapel from the bones of their pre-deceased brothers would be horrified at such disrespect: the Chapel of the Bones belongs to a southern European tradition of reminding onlookers of their mortality and shocking them into a more sober and upright life. Perhaps the intended *memento mori* effect (the inscription over the entrance translates as 'Stop here and think of the fate that will befall you') would have been better achieved by a less decorous arrangement of skeletal remains. As it is, the chapel, completed in 1816, is too neat and tidy to be macabre, with legs and arm bones used to create a classical architectural arrangement of arches, capitals and pilasters.

It is worth taking some time to look at the church to which the chapel is attached. The Igreja do Carmo was built in 1719 and has an imposing baroque façade, flanked by twin bell-towers – its ancient grandeur now somewhat compromised by its setting amongst modern tower blocks. Both the main altar and the side altars are decorated in the typical Portuguese baroque style known as *talha dourada*, with extravagantly carved and gilded woodwork, featuring scores of cherubs playing amongst acanthus leaf and vine foliage.

Historically, the church has played an important role, for in 1808 it was here that the people of Faro met, under the pretence of holding a normal religious service, to plot their ultimately successful resistance to the Napoleonic occupation of the town.

6
Castelo de Silves

The Algarve's best-preserved castle symbolises the splendour of Silves in its Moorish heyday.

The streets of Silves were once packed with traders, bazaars overflowed with exotic goods, and the gilded domes of many minarets gleamed in the sun. The bustling capital of 12th-century Moorish Algarve, known as Xelb, is today a sleepy place with 12,000 inhabitants. Only the castle indicates the town's former wealth and importance.

The castle was built to last and, despite bearing the brunt of fighting during the Christian Reconquest of Portugal in the 12th and 13th centuries, it remains substantially intact. Following the rampart walk, you can take in views over the roof-tops of the town to the River Arade, once the site of a bustling harbour, and across countryside planted with the orange, almond and carob trees which the Moors introduced.

Excavations continue to uncover the castle's secrets: recently exposed walls show the remains of earlier Phoenician and Roman fortifications and vestiges of the palace of the Moorish rulers. Near by, the domed cistern is still used as a reservoir for the town's water supply. This same cistern kept the castle's Moorish inhabitants alive for six weeks during the 1189 Siege of Silves. When the Moors finally surrendered, the Crusaders went on an orgy of looting, confident that the Moors would soon be driven from the Iberian Peninsula. Their joy was shortlived: Moorish forces from Seville returned to exact revenge, and it was another 60 years before Afonso III finally brought the Algarve back to Christianity.

28C2

Largo do Castelo, Silves

282 445624

Summer daily 9–7; Winter daily 9–6. Last entry ½ hour before closing. Closed public hols

Cafés (£) near castle entrance and alongside the cathedral, including Café Inglês (£, ► 95)

Few

Moderate

Historic centre and museums of Silves (► 44–45)

Bigger than the town it protects – the Castle of the Moors at Silves

7
Estói

29E2

Rua da Barroca, Estói

289 997282

Tue–Sat 9–12:30, 2–5:30. Closed Sun, Mon and public hols

Sol Algarvio (£) and Ossonoba (£) opposite the church

Few

Free

Vila Romana de Milreu (➤ 24)

Decades of neglect have only added to the charm and appeal of the palace garden in Estói.

Behind high walls, in the little village of Estói, lies a lavish rococo palace, built in the 18th century for the Conde de Carvalhal. The family wealth declined, and the palace was acquired by Faro city council some years ago, the plan being to restore the building for use as a *pousada* (a state-run luxury hotel). The building remains empty and much of the grounds are off limits but the main entranceway from the church square leads down a cobbled road to the heart of the complex for wonderful views of the outer façade and tantalising glimpses across the faded grandeur of the formal garden, with its palm-lined avenues and terraces.

Designed to please the senses, the walls of the garden are decorated with *azulejos* depicting bucolic scenes of

shepherds and shepherdesses, while naked youths frolic with dolphins in the fountains. Elsewhere, buxom goddesses drape themselves langorously around water-filled shells, against a tiled background of cranes and bullrushes. On the lower terrace, a stone-lined nymphaeum shelters a copy of Canova's famous statue *The Three Graces,* flanked by ornate mosaics.

Climb the ornate stairway to the upper entrance courtyard from where you'll get the best views of the palace itself, the soft pink hue of the walls deepens as the sun drops and there are innumerable decorative details to admire. Regular visitors would probably prefer Estói to be kept this way, as they have come to love the softened outlines of crumbling balustrades, the crooked steps and loose cobbles, and the ghostly atmosphere.

Nymphs at their ease (inset) in Estói's aristocratic gardens

8
Milreu

Exploring the extensive remains of the Roman villa at Milreu demonstrates how little life in the Algarve has changed.

Dancing dolphins grace Milreu's Roman pools, spas and baths

29E2

On the western outskirts of Estói, well signposted from main approach roads

Tue–Sun 9:30–12:30; 2–6 (until 5 Oct–Apr). Closed Mon and public hols

Cafés (£) in front of parish church

Few

Moderate

Palácio de Estói (➤ 22)

Junta de Freguesia
☎ 289 991620

At Milreu, you will discover that wealthy Romans enjoyed houses that are not so different, in many respects, from today's luxurious holiday homes.

The villa was probably built by a 1st-century AD fish magnate – perhaps the owner of a fish-processing factory, where locally caught sardines, tuna and swordfish were dried and salted before being packed in barrels for export. This theory is based on the fact that the wonderful mosaics that decorate many of the rooms show fish leaping in and out of the frothy waves. These denizens of the deep adorn the walls and rooms on both sides of the villa – the bath house to the left (west), with its hot and cold pools and its hypocaust system for providing under-floor heating, and the living quarters, to the right (east). Separating the two is a large courtyard garden which was once surrounded by a shady pillared colonnade.

Another plausible theory is that this was not a private villa at all, but a spa and temple complex. The huge building that survives to roof height to the east of the site is interpreted as a nymphaeum, a shrine to the local water nymphs, which was converted for use as a church in the early Christian period, reusing the pools and piscinas as baptismal fonts. Visitors coming to worship at this shrine would have used the bath facilities, which are somewhat grand just for a private villa. The sheer number of stone cubicles in the *apodyterium* (changing room) alongside the bath complex would seem to support the theory that this was a public facility – unless the owner was in the habit of throwing lavish poolside parties!

9
Ponta da Piedade

Consider taking a trip by boat to explore the spectacular free-standing pillars, rock stacks and grottoes of this cove near Lagos.

For coastal scenery, the coves around Ponta da Piedade are hard to beat. The same geological processes and erosive forces that carved out the rock sculptures at Algar Seco (➤ 16) have been at work here too, creating a coastline of ochre and rust-red cliffs, stacks and arches, which resemble the ruins of some fantasy castle.

From the cliff-tops at Ponta da Piedade you can walk along a path to the various sea grottoes (➤ 33), but the going can be precarious. From the lighthouse at Ponta da Piedade, for example, there are paths ranging all along the coastline with views to the foaming waters below, but vertigo sufferers may find it a problem. There is also a set of steps descending the cliff face from the lighthouse down to a rock platform where local fishermen wait to take passengers on short coastal trips to see the cliffs between here and Praia da Luz. This is well worth doing, especially during the nesting season, when you may get a good close-up of cliff-nesting birds, such as the heron-like cattle egrets and little egrets.

Another option is to join one of the boat trips that depart regularly from Lagos, such as those operated by Bom Dia. Trips usually last from 10 until 2, or from 2:30 to 6, but full-day trips are available as well, allowing time for swimming, snorkelling and lunch on board ship.

28B2

2km south of Lagos

Bar Sol Nascante (£), opposite the lighthouse

Bom Dia Actividades Marítimas
Marina de Lagos
282 764670
Office: 9–6 in winter; 9–9 in summer. Closed Jan and Feb. Cruises: daily, plus sunset cruises in summer departing 7:30PM

Free

Historic centre and museums of Lagos (➤ 32–34)

Looking down to turquoise waters between Ponta da Piedade's rock stacks

10 Reserva Natural da Ria Formosa

29E1

Visitor centre: 1km east of Olhão, signposted to the Parque Natural, and *campismo* (campsite)

Visitor centre: Mon–Fri 9–12:30, 2–5:30. Closed Sat, Sun and public hols

Small café at the visitor centre; plenty of choice in Olhão (£–££)

Olhão (► 86)

Learn all about the wildlife of the Algarve's lagoons, and meet an unusual breed of poodle.

The Ria Formosa Nature Reserve stretches for some 30km along the coast, from Ançāo, west of Faro, to Manta Rota, near the Spanish border. It consists of scores of sandy islands, linked by shallow lagoons, salt marshes and water channels, which are home to birds, plants and insects. While the outer islands facing the Atlantic bear the brunt of oceanic wind and waves, these shallow lagoons are warm and sheltered, providing perfect spawning conditions for many fish, and an ideal feeding ground for birds.

The best place for getting acquainted with the complex ecology of the reserve is at the visitor centre at Quinta do Marim, 1km east of Olhão. Displays provide information on conservation activities and wildlife, and maps can be obtained showing recommended walking routes. You can also enquire about visiting the kennels where the rare Portuguese water dog, the Cão de Água, is bred to save it from extinction. These endearing 'poodles', with big limbs and curly black hair, have web-like membranes between their paws which enable them to swim very effectively. Algarvian fishermen once trained the dogs to help them by diving and shepherding fish into their nets.

Two areas of the reserve are readily accessible by boat: ferries depart from the harbour in Olhão to the Ilha da Armona (daily at 8:30, 12 and 5; last boat back at 5:30), and to Farol, on the Ilha da Culatra (daily 11, 3 and 6:30; last boat back at 7:15). From these sand spits you can watch the bird life of the lagoons, or find your own private strip of unspoilt beach and sand dune for sunbathing.

Sea life flourishes in the sheltered lagoons of the Ria Formosa

What to See

Above: *enjoy a drink in Lagos*
Right: *a Salema fisherman mends his nets*

Aljezur's sugar-cube houses are built in the Moorish style

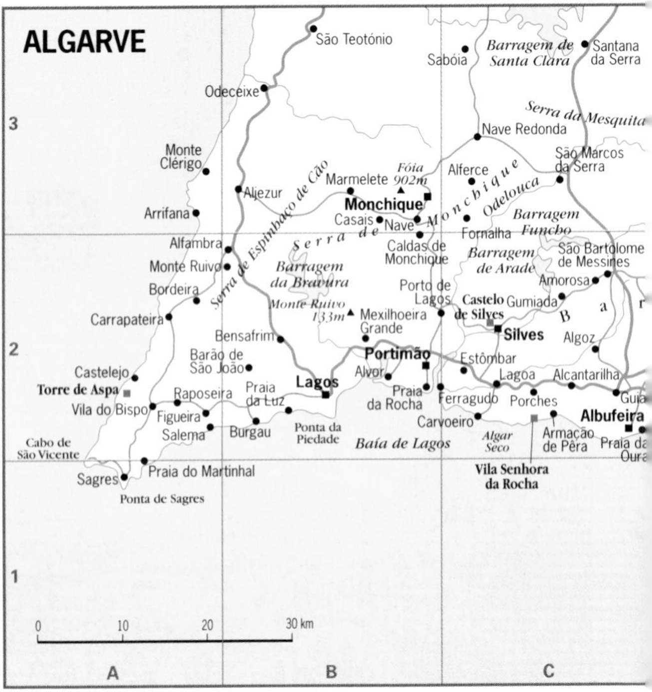

ALGARVE

São Teotónio
Sabóia
Barragem de Santa Clara
Santana da Serra
Odeceixe
Serra da Mesquita
Nave Redonda
Monte Clérigo
São Marcos da Serra
Aljezur
Marmelete
Fóia 902m
Alferce
Monchique
Serra de Espinhaço de Cão
Serra de Monchique
Odelouca
Arrifana
Casais
Nave
Barragem Funcho
Fornalha
Alfambra
Caldas de Monchique
Barragem de Arade
São Bartolome de Messines
Monte Ruivo
Barragem da Bravura
Bordeira
Porto de Lagos
Amorosa
Monte Ruivo 133m
Mexilhoeira Grande
Castelo de Silves
Gumiada
Carrapateira
Silves
Algoz
Bensafrim
Portimão
Barão de São João
Estômbar
Castelejo
Alvor
Lagoa
Alcantarilha
Torre de Aspa
Lagos
Praia da Luz
Raposeira
Praia da Rocha
Ferragudo
Porches
Vila do Bispo
Figueira
Carvoeiro
Albufeira
Salema
Burgau
Ponta da Piedade
Algar Seco
Armação de Pêra
Praia da Oura
Guia
Cabo de São Vicente
Baía de Lagos
Praia do Martinhal
Vila Senhora da Rocha
Sagres
Ponta de Sagres
0 10 20 30 km
A B C
1 2 3

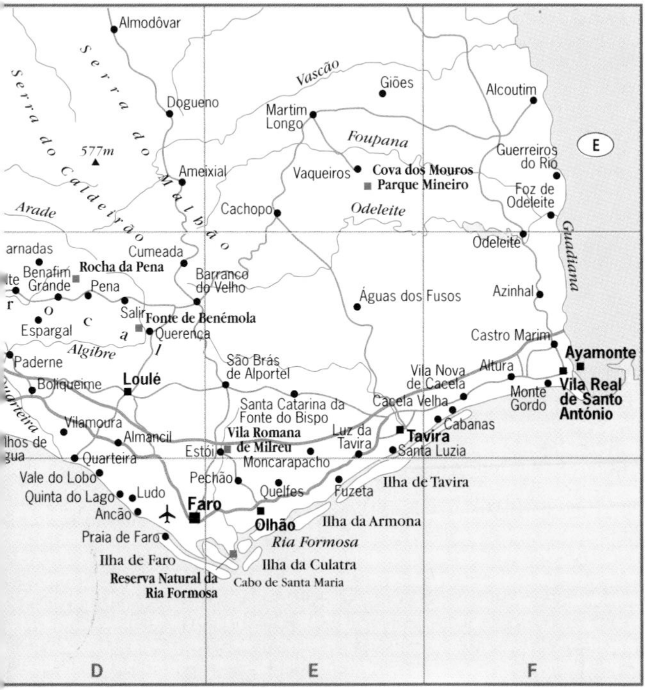

Almodôvar
Serra do Malhão
Serra do Caldeirão
Vascão
Giões
Alcoutim
Dogueno
Martim Longo
Foupana
577m
Guerreiros do Rio
E
Ameixial
Vaqueiros
Cova dos Mouros
Parque Mineiro
Foz de Odeleite
Arade
Cachopo
Odeleite
Odeleite
Guadiana
arnadas
Cumeada
Benafim Grande
Rocha da Pena
Barranco do Velho
Pena
Azinhal
Águas dos Fusos
Salir
Fonte de Benémola
Espargal
Querença
Castro Marim
Algibre
Paderne
São Brás de Alportel
Ayamonte
Altura
Loulé
Vila Nova de Cacela
Boliqueime
Monte Gordo
Vila Real de Santo António
Santa Catarina da Fonte do Bispo
Cacela Velha
Vilamoura
Cabanas
Vila Romana de Milreu
Luz da Tavira
Tavira
Almancil
Estói
Santa Luzia
Quarteira
Moncarapacho
Vale do Lobo
Pechão
Ilha de Tavira
Quinta do Lago
Ludo
Quelfes
Fuzeta
Faro
Ancão
Olhão
Ilha da Armona
Praia de Faro
Ria Formosa
Ilha de Faro
Ilha da Culatra
Reserva Natural da Ria Formosa
Cabo de Santa Maria
D
E
F

Western Algarve

To the people of 15th-century Portugal, the western shores of the Algarve represented the end of the civilised world – beyond lay only uncertainty. Today, and even in the finest weather, the wave-battered cliffs of Cabo de São Vicente (Cape St Vincent) can appear suitably apocalyptic, and the Costa Vicentina, that part of the Algarvian coast that faces west on to the full force of the Atlantic, has some of the finest surfing beaches in Europe.

The west, being furthest from Faro airport, and lacking the long sandy beaches of the east, remains the least developed part of coastal Algarve, and is the part that appeals most to visitors in search of tranquillity, wildlife and the opportunity to experience Portuguese culture relatively untouched by the trappings of mass tourism.

'Where the land ends and the sea begins.'

LUÍS DE CAMÕES,
describing the Algarve in
his epic narrative
The Lusiads (1572)

Portugal's Atlantic coast offers some of Europe's wildest waves

28B2
Lagos railway station ☎ 282 762987, 1km north of the town centre
Bus terminus: Rossio de São João ☎ 282 762944, with services to and from Aljezur, Burgau, Odeceixe, Portimão, Sagres, Salema and Vila do Bispo
Luz (➤ 36)
Rua Vasco da Gama, São João ☎ 282 763031

Lagos

Lagos is an atmospheric town encircled by massive 16th-century walls that effectively shut out the 21st century, including the western Algarve's biggest concentration of hotel developments to the west of the town. Holidaymakers tire of the beach and drift into Lagos to discover a maze of cobbled streets, too narrow for cars to penetrate. Café owners have set up tables and chairs, tempting visitors to stop and sample their delicious coffee and cakes, in between exploring the town's churches, museums, art galleries, antique shops and bustling market.

Lagos harbour saw the start of many voyages of discovery

Parking spaces are available along the Avenida dos Descobrimentos, the palm-lined road that runs alongside the River Bensafrim. Sheltered from the open sea, the river was adapted for use as a canal to provide access to the town's harbour. Sleek white yachts and battered fishing boats sit side by side in the modern harbour, and signs point the way to the offices of companies offering fishing trips and voyages to the caves and coves of Ponta da Piedade (➤ 25, 113).

The social hub of Lagos lies at Praça Gil Eanes, with a huge statue of Dom Sebastião at the centre of the square. This modern statue (1973), the work of sculptor João Cutileiro, portrays Prince Sebastian, who believed it was his mission to conquer North Africa and convert the Moors to Christianity. He gathered an army of 18,000 men and set sail from Lagos in 1578. When his ill-equipped army met a vastly superior force at Alcacer-Quibir, in Morocco, only 100 Portuguese survivors emerged from the battle to tell the tale.

From Lagos to Luz

Distance
6km (1.5km from Praia Dona Ana to Ponta da Piedade)

Time
3 hours (long walk); 30 minutes (short walk)

Start point
Municipal tourist information centre, Largo Marquês de Pombal, in Lagos, or the Praia Dona Ana car park
✚ 28B2

End point
Luz
✚ 28B2

Lunch
O Poço (££)
✉ Avenida dos Pescadores, Luz
☎ 282 789189

Early evening is a good time for this walk, when you can enjoy the setting sun. Ambitious walkers can take the whole route from Lagos to Luz and back; alternatively you can take the bus one way and walk back – check the times of buses between Lagos and Luz at the tourist information centre in Lagos. A third option, which is ideal for walkers with children, is to take the much shorter route to Ponta da Piedade and back.

Start from the centre of Lagos by walking west along the Avenida dos Descobrimentos, past the Forte da Ponta da Bandeira (➤ 34). Following the main road uphill and out of the town, turn left at the sign to Praia de Dona Ana at the first set of traffic lights. If you have a car, start at Praia de Dona Ana, leaving the car in the car park on the cliff-tops above the beach.

Explore the beach at Praia de Dona Ana, where the rocks are like fossilised sponge, then climb back up and take the cliff-top path that leads south.

Goats and walkers have eroded a number of tracks at this point, but they all lead in the same direction. Continue southwards, keeping the sea on your left, until you reach Ponta da Piedade.

At Ponta da Piedade, you will find fishermen waiting to take visitors on short trips to the nearby grottoes.

From Ponta da Piedade, the path turns westward and follows the cliff-tops. Porto de Mós, with its beach and café, is reached after about 20 minutes. From here, a track continues westwards, levelling out on the cliff-tops, and continuing for some 50 minutes to Luz.

The most prominent feature in the landscape is the *atalaia* (obelisk) above Luz, which marks the highest point (109m) reached by the cliffs on this stretch of coast.

A typical rock formation at Praia de Dona Ana

What to See in Lagos

FORTE DA PONTA DA BANDEIRA ✪

Cais de Solaria
Tue–Sun 9:30–12:30, 2–5. Closed Mon and public hols
Moderate

This 17th-century moated fortress was built to defend the town and port. Reached by a bridge and impressive gatehouse, it contains a small maritime museum, documenting the place of Lagos in the Age of Discovery.

MERCADO DOS ESCRAVOS (SLAVE MARKET) ✪✪

Praça da República
Few
Free

Though not much to look at, this covered arcade, below the Customs House on the eastern side of Praça da República, is of great historical importance, for it was here, in 1444, that modern Europe's first slave market was established. Despite this, Portugal was the first nation to abolish slavery, as part of the humanistic reforms of the Marquês de Pombal (► 88) in the 1750s.

PONTA DA PIEDADE (► 25, TOP TEN)

SANTO ANTÓNIO AND MUSEU MUNICIPAL ✪✪✪

Rua General Alberto da Silveira
282 762301
Tue–Sun 9:30–12:30, 2–5. Closed Mon and public hols
Moderate (one ticket gives entry to both sights)

The Igreja de Santo António is one of the most lavishly decorated churches in the Algarve. Early 18th-century carved and gilded woodwork covers the entire east wall and frames wall paintings depicting scenes from the life of St Anthony, a Franciscan friar and native of Portugal, who devoted his life to care of the poor.

The adjoining Municipal Museum is packed with curiosities. Religious artefacts such as vestments and baroque paintings form an important part of the collection, but the timeline runs from prehistoric pottery to Roman statuary found at Milreu (► 24) and pre-World War II German banknotes. There is also an interesting display of Portuguese chimney pots, showing regional differences.

Above: *scenes from the Life of St Anthony, set in lavish frames of carved wood and gold*

What to See in Western Algarve

ALJEZUR

Aljezur is the largest town on the scenic N120 road to Lisbon. High on the hill above Aljezur are the ruins of the massive 10th-century Moorish castle, captured by Dom Paio Peres Correia in 1246. He is said to have charmed a beautiful Moorish maiden who opened the castle doors to him one moonlit night. Good beaches near by include Arrifana (10km southwest), and Amoreira/Monte Clérigo (8km northwest). Some 17km north, the pretty, pottery-producing village of Odeceixe stands beside the river that marks the boundary between the Algarve and the Alentejo.

28B3
30km northwest of Lagos
Café (£) in Largo 5 de Outubro
Irregular bus service from Lagos
Monchique (► 50)
Estrada Nacional
282 998229

BURGAU

Burgau stands on the southeastern edge of the Costa Vicentina Nature Park, which extends in a broad sweep north from here to Odeceixe. The park encompasses 80km of coastline, whose poor soils and windswept salt-laden air have prevented farming and left an untamed landscape in which wildlife thrives – especially birds of prey and wading birds. Burgau makes an excellent base for exploring this region, with a good choice of accommodation in the village.

28B2
12km west of Lagos
Ponta de Almadena (£); several more on the seafront at Burgau (£)
Bus from Lagos
Lagos (► 32)

Bringing home the catch at Burgau

CABO DE SÃO VICENTE (► 18, TOP TEN)

CARRAPATEIRA 

Sleepy Carrapateira owes its popularity to its proximity to some of the west coast's best beaches (► 41). West of the town is Bordeira, guarded by the ruins of a 17th-century fortress and backed by huge dunes and a lagoon. Amado, further south, has the so-called Pedra do Cavaleiro (Knight's Rock) to protect it. The thundering surf all along the coast here appeals to watersports enthusiasts, but the landscape of towering cliffs and miles of sand is just as attractive for walkers and photographers.

28A2
35km northwest of Lagos
Small café (£) in main square
Bus from Lagos
Lagos (► 32)

LUZ ✪✪

- 28B2
- 8km west of Lagos
- Numerous cafés, including the Kiwi (£) on Avenida do Pescadores; Fortaleza da Luz (££)
- Bus from Lagos
- Few
- Lagos (➤ 32)

Luz marks the westernmost point of tourist development in the Algarve, and is an excellent base for family holidays. The holiday village here has won praise and awards for sensitive development: the whitewashed villas, dripping with scarlet and purple bougainvillaea, echo the shapes and colours of the older houses that line the road to the picturesque beach, and blend harmoniously with the natural topography. The sheltered beach at Praia da Luz has rock pools to explore, and a number of artificial scoops cut from the rocks that have been claimed as ancient (pre-Roman) tanks for salting and curing fish. At the height of the main season there is a well-organised watersports school and sea-sport centre in the village offering facilities and tuition for sailing, diving and windsurfing.

From the beach there are cliff-top paths to explore (➤ 33), including one to the east of the village, which climbs to the Miradouro da Atalaia. Here an obelisk marks 109m above sea level, and offers sweeping coastal views. At the other end of the village is a 17th-century fortress which has now been turned into a popular restaurant. Near by, the village church has a pre-earthquake Gothic chancel, decorated with elaborate, 18th-century gilded carving.

Luz, with its well-planned mixture of old and new

SAGRES ✪✪✪

Sagres is Europe's most southwesterly community. Just 6km east of Cabo de São Vicente (► 18), it sits atop a rocky plateau, scoured by the same winds that send the sea crashing against the rocks of the nearby beaches. Even more bleak is the promontory south of the town, the site of the **Fortaleza (Fortress) de Sagres**, where Prince Henry the Navigator established his school of seamanship in 1443.

The sailors who came to study here lived an almost monastic life as they prepared to sail to new worlds, having mastered astronomy, navigation and cartography. The walls of the small town that Henry had built on the cliff-tops still survive, offering superb views across the rocky promontory, as does the simple chapel, with its altarpiece depicting St Vincent holding a ship (currently under renovation). Near by is a 15th-century Rosa dos Ventos (wind rose) inscribed into the rock, 43m in diameter, which may once have been fitted with a weather vane to indicate the wind direction. The Vila do Infante, where Prince Henry lived, along with many other original buildings, was destroyed by the English buccaneer Sir Francis Drake in 1587, when Portugal was under Spanish rule.

Although the modern town has little to hold the attention, there are compensations to living in Sagres, including pristine coves to explore. Local fishermen keep the restaurants well supplied with fresh fish and seafood, and also offer boat trips to view the magnificent Costa Vicentina from the sea. There are many cliff-top walks, and in spring and autumn you can watch migrating birds flying over the headland or wheeling past the cliffs.

28A1

32km west of Lagos

Numerous cafés (£) around main square; Fortaleza do Beliche (££), on road from Sagres to Cabo de São Vicente

Bus from Lagos

Rua Comandante Matoso
282 624873

Cabo de São Vicente (► 18)

Fortaleza de Sagres

Ponta de Sagres

Summer 10–8:30; winter 10–6:30. Closed 1 May and 25 Dec

Expensive

Few

Below: *pointing to all corners of the globe – the wind rose at Sagres*

In the Know

If you only have a short time to visit the Algarve, or would like to get a real flavour of the region, here are some ideas:

Hot and spicy chicken piri-piri, *influenced by North African cuisine*

10 Ways to Be a Local

Visit a café and order a *bica* (strong black espresso coffee) for breakfast, accompanied by sweet pastries.

Greet shopkeepers and café proprietors with a cheery *bom dia, boa tarde* or *boa noite* (good morning, afternoon and evening) as you enter and leave.

Buy lunch in one of the covered markets or shop early for tasty, freshly baked bread and the best choice of fruit, flowers and fish.

Join the fishermen on the beach at Monte Gordo or Salema, and watch them sorting out their day's catch.

Stay up late talking to friends over a drink in a seafront café.

Catch up on lost sleep by taking a long siesta after lunch, waking up in time to join friends for an early evening stroll around town.

Listen to *fado* in any of the bars and hotels that specialise in this unique Portuguese form of music (➤ 112).

Look for bunting strung across village streets – a sign there will be a festival at the weekend.

Discover the secret of eternal youth by drinking fresh spring water at any of the Algarve's spas, such as Caldas de Monchique or Alte.

Find your own desert island, or at least your own private stretch of beach, by taking a ferry from Olhão to one of the barrier islands in the Ria Formosa lagoon (➤ 26).

10 Good Places to Have Lunch

Burgau Beach Bar (£), Burgau (➤ 92).

Café Alianca (£), Praça Francisco Gomes 6, Faro ☎ 289 801621. Forgive the slow service – the décor and ambience is the reason for being here, in the dimly lit interior of one of Portugal's oldest cafés.

Fortaleza da Luz (££), Luz (➤ 93).

Imperial (£££), Tavira (➤ 99).

Mediterraneo (£), Lagos (➤ 93).

O Pescador (££) ✉ Rua Comandante Matoso, Baleeira, near Sagres ☎ 282 624192. Enjoy some of the freshest and best seafood in Western Algarve – try *cataplana*, seafood rice or grilled swordfish.

O Soeiro (£), Alcoutim (➤ 98).

Cafés are a second home, and the centre of Algarvian social life

Paraíso da Montanha (£), Monchique (➤ 95).
Restaurant Casa do Golfe (£££), Quinta do Lago (➤ 97).
Termas de Monchique (£££), Caldas de Monchique (➤ 94).

10 Activities

Birdwatching: the lagoons and wetland marshes attract wading birds big and small, from shy flamingos and stilts to storks, herons and egrets.
Fishing: join a deep-sea fishing expedition and pit your wits against such game fish as swordfish, marlin and shark.
Golf: the Algarve is renowned for its scenic courses; why not sign up for a session with the resident pro?
Horse riding: beginners and children are welcome at any of the Algarve's growing number of stables, for a scenic forest or coastal ride.
Hunting for wild flowers: you cannot visit the Algarve in spring or early summer without being impressed by nature's profusion (but remember not to pick wild flowers).
Keeping fit: make the most of the sports facilities to tone up your muscles, improve your golf handicap or perfect your tennis.
Sailing: with its many private coves and marine grottoes, the western Algarve is an ideal place to enjoy a short coastal voyage.
Shopping for souvenirs: head for Loulé (➤ 108) for a good selection of crafts, or browse the pottery workshops of Porches (➤ 106) for a colourful hand-painted plate.
Walking: from forests to cliff-tops, from mountains to riverbanks, the Algarve is ideal walking country – buy the Sunflower walking guide for ideas (➤ 12).
Watersports: learn to dive or windsurf with one of the several licensed diving and watersports schools.

5 Top Souvenir Ideas

- Almond fruits – delicious almond paste sculpted to look like apples, pears or strawberries.
- A *cataplana* cooking pot so that you can re-create typical Portuguese stews at home.
- A large decorative bowl painted with flowers or fruits.
- Leather sandals, shoes or bags at bargain prices.
- A lace tablecloth or shawl bought in a street market.

5 Good Viewpoints

- Alcoutim castle (➤ 80)
- Aljezur castle (➤ 35)
- Cabo de São Vicente (➤ 18)
- The peak of Fóia mountain (➤ 59)
- Silves castle (➤ 21)

Decorative pottery

28A2
15km west of Lagos
Several cafés and bars (£) in Rua dos Pescadores
Bus from Lagos
Few
Lagos (➤ 32)

Salema's fishermen offer coastal tours to view the bird life

SALEMA 

Despite the shops, bars and restaurants catering for visitors, Salema still has the air of an unspoiled coastal village, where the fishermen haul in their catch by the first light of dawn. Several offer fishing excursions to visitors, supplying tackle, tuition for beginners and lunch. Equally popular are birdwatching excursions into the marshes west of the village. For sun worshippers, there is a sheltered beach at Ponta de Almadena, and another at neighbouring Boca do Rio; the two are linked by a 2km cliff-top walk.

28A2
22km west of Lagos
Cafés (£) around Praça da República
Bus from Lagos
Few
Lagos (➤ 32)

VILA DO BISPO 

Vila do Bispo (Bishop's Town) was renamed after this former royal town was given to the Bishop of Algarve by King Manuel I in 1515. It was a rich prize, for the bishop enjoyed the revenues from the town's many windmills. Today only a couple of white windmills remain, minus their sails, and the structure that now dominates the horizon is a massive water tower. Near by is the 18th-century parish church, Nossa Senhora da Conceição, decorated with *azulejos* depicting dolphins, and dating from 1726. It also has a fine painted roof, and the sacristy serves as a small museum, displaying 16th-century painted panels and statues of saints.

Nearby Raposeira, 1km to the east, has a house that claims to be a former residence of Henry the Navigator. From the same period are the Manueline doorways of the parish church, its pyramid-roofed bell-tower and the chancel arch. Even older is the Chapel of Nossa Senhora de Guadalupe (private property), to the north of the N125, east of Figueira, which dates from the 13th century and may have been built for the crusading Knights Templar.

Western Highlights

The scenery on this drive varies from fishing ports and wave-battered cliffs to river valleys and sandy beaches.

Head northwest on the N120, over the Serra de Espinhaço de Cão foothills, to Aljezur.

Climb to the Aljezur castle (➤ 35) and then cool off on the wonderful beach at Arrifana, where you can explore the ruins of an old coastal fort and look out to the Pedra da Agulha (Needle Rock) at the end of the cliffs.

Head south on the N268 towards Vila do Bispo (➤ 40). Just north of Carrapateira, take the right turn at the O Cabrita restaurant and follow the coast road for a dramatic tour past Bordeira and Amado beaches and the rugged cliffs that separate them.

Stay for a swim or stroll if time allows. This is one of the most dramatic routes in the Costa Vicentina Nature Park and it leads back to the main road south of town, from where you can continue your journey.

Continue on the N268 southwards to Sagres.

From here you can visit Cabo de São Vicente (➤ 18), or Ponta de Sagres (➤ 37), to see the site of Henry the Navigator's school of seamanship.

Return to Vila do Bispo, and take the N125 east, towards Lagos.

Stop at Vila do Bispo for its church and the Nossa Senhora de Guadalupe chapel, beyond Raposeira.

About 3km beyond Raposeira, turn right to follow roads (some of them unmetalled but well maintained) through Figueira, Salema, Burgau and Luz.

Look out for birds as you go, and pick any of the beaches en route for a dip – or walk on the cliff paths above Luz. Alternatively, end the day at Praia de Dona Ana (➤ 33), watching the sunset from the cliff-tops.

Distance
120km

Time
6 hours

Start/end point
Lagos
28B2

Lunch
O Pescador (££)
Rua Comandante Matoso, Baleeira, south of Sagres
282 624192

On the western coast you will often have the beach to yourself

Western Central Algarve

Between Lagos in the west and Albufeira in the east, western central Algarve takes in a stretch of coast that combines attractive resorts with port towns, where catering to tourism takes second place to fishing and fish processing. Inland lies Porches, the centre of the Algarvian pottery industry, and Silves, a majestic hilltown with enough history to satisfy any culture-seeking visitor.

Beyond the fertile valleys around Silves lie the foothills of the Serra de Monchique. Here two huge reservoirs trap rainfall and spring water, supplying the region's drinking water and providing recreational facilities for anglers and boating enthusiasts. Northwards again are the pretty villages of the Monchique mountains, offering cool summer retreats from the baking-hot coast, and miles of tree-shaded footpaths, as well as the Algarve's highest peak, at Fóia (902m).

'Protected by a strong wall, [Silves] possesses a port and shipyard and is fine in appearance, with attractive buildings and well-furnished bazaars.'

IDRISI
12th-century Arab chronicler

Sculpted cliffs and coloured sands are the trademark of Praia da Rocha

Silves

28C2

Railway station 2km south of town

Bus terminus alongside Mercado Municipal 282 442338, with services to and from Albufeira, Armação de Pêra, Lagoa, Messines, Monchique and Portimão

Rua 25 de Abril 282 442255

Portimão (➤ 52)

Silves is a compact town built on a series of terraces between the River Arade and the massive castle. One way to approach the town is by sailing upriver from Portimão (➤ 113 for details of river cruises) following the same route taken by Phoenician traders who established their base here in the 1st millennium BC. Their riverside colony grew to become the Roman city of Silbis, and then, from the 8th century, the Moorish city of Xelb. Described by Arabic chroniclers as 10 times more impressive than Lisbon, Xelb was a city of gleaming domes and minarets, of poets, writers and musicians, traders, craftsmen and farmers.

Due to the earthquake of 1755, little now survives of the Arabic influence – at least in architectural terms. The most lasting legacy is visible in the almond and citrus groves that you see as you look down from the castle walls (➤ 21) across the surrounding countryside. It was the Moors who introduced these crops, along with the irrigation system.

From the castle, narrow cobbled streets descend steeply to the cathedral and the archaeological museum. From the museum it is a short stroll through the Torreão das Portas da Cidade, the medieval town gate, to the main

The stones of Silves tell the story of the town's Moorish past

square, the Praça do Municipio, with its town hall, ancient pillory and pavement cafés. Shop-lined streets lead from here down to the covered market and the embankments of the River Arade, where pavement cafés offer views of the town's medieval bridge.

What to See in Silves

CASTELO (➤ 21, TOP TEN)

CRUZ DE PORTUGAL ✪

Sited beside a busy roundabout on the northeastern entrance to the city, the Cross of Portugal is a beautiful religious sculpture dating from the early 16th century. Such crosses were erected at key points along medieval pilgrim routes and this is a rare surviving example.

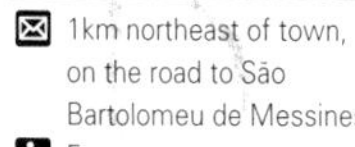
1km northeast of town, on the road to São Bartolomeu de Messines

Few

Free

FÁBRICA DO INGLÊS AND MUSEU DA CORTIÇA ✪✪

A cork factory near the river has been transformed into a leisure complex – Fábrica do Inglês – with gallery space, restaurants, street entertainment and a water show with lights and music. The complex features a Cork Museum, celebrating one of Portugal's most important exports.

Rua Gregório Mascarenhas

282 440480; www.fabrica-do-ingles.com

Apr–Oct daily 10–10; Nov–Mar daily 10–5

MUSEU MUNICIPAL DE ARQUEOLOGIA ✪✪

The archaeological museum is built around the excavated remains of a Moorish house. The complexity and beauty of the well, with its stone flagged spiral staircase lit by arched windows, descending to the watery depths, makes you realise how impressive the Moorish city must have been. The museum explains the city's evolution from prehistoric to recent times. The top floor leads out on to a restored section of the city wall, from where there is a view down over the old Moorish quarter.

Rua das Portas de Loulé 14

282 444832

Mon–Sat 9–6. Closed public hols

Good

Moderate

SÉ (CATHEDRAL) ✪✪✪

Built on the site of the Moorish mosque to symbolise the expulsion of the Moors from the city, the magnificent 13th- to 15th-century cathedral is one of only a few in the Algarve to retain its medieval feel. Free from the gilded baroque woodwork of many post-earthquake churches, the rose-pink granite columns and vaults soar above the tombs of medieval knights and bishops.

Rua da Sé

Daily 8:30–6:30

Few

Free

What to See in Western Central Algarve

ALGAR SECO (➤ 16, TOP TEN)

28C2
9km northeast of Armação de Pêra
Restaurante O João
282 575332
Bus from Armação de Pêra or Portimão
Albufeira (➤ 66)

ALGOZ

This fast expanding village, centred around a core of modest whitewashed houses, has two churches worth visiting. The 18th-century parish church has a baptistery replete with *azulejos* and statues still paraded through the streets on feast days. On a small hill above the village is the Hermitage of Nossa Senhora do Pilar, whose interior contains 18th-century paintings of the Stations of the Cross. The panoramic views across the valley from the hermitage have been somewhat spoilt by a new factory near by.

28B2
4km west of Portimão
Àbabuja (££)
Bus from Portimão
Albufeira (➤ 66)

ALVOR

Alvor is situated on the eastern edge of the wide Baia de Lagos (Lagos Bay), a shallow, bird-filled lagoon formed by the estuary of four rivers. Fishing was the inspiration behind the carvings that decorate the portal of the 16th-century parish church. Local fishermen join the wading birds in the tidal estuary, searching for razor shells and clams, which are sold in the fish market on the harbour, and which form the principal ingredient of the seafood dishes served in local bars and restaurants. For a closer look at the lagoon, it is best to follow the raised footpath that winds between the salt pans close to the shore.

A swathe of land west of the town has been commandeered by several large modern hotel complexes, with development reaching all the way to Praia de Alvor and Praia dos Três Irmãos and almost filling the gap between Alvor and Praia da Rocha (➤ 53). The hotels are well placed for days on the beach or the relative bustle of nearby Portimão and Lagos.

Fresh fish straight from the sea and grilled to perfection

Did you know ?

King João II died in Alvor in 1495. Dropsy was given as the official cause of his death, but many suspected that he was poisoned by Spaniards, intent on the conquest of Portugal.

Vertical cliffs enclose a perfect cove at Senhora da Rocha

ARMAÇÃO DE PÊRA

Armação de Pêra is a burgeoning resort full of multi-storey apartment blocks and hotels, sprawling along a broad stretch of sandy beach that marks the watershed between the rocky coves of the western Algarve and the sandy shores of the east. Visitors can laze on the sands within sight of the colourfully painted boats belonging to the local fishing fleet, or engage in the many activities on offer, such as surfing at Vale de Centianes, or snorkelling at Marinha or Albandeira.

Nearby Senhora da Rocha has adjacent bays sheltered by high cliffs, between hotel complexes. Perched high on the cliff above is the delightful Ermida de Nossa Senhora da Rocha (Hermitage of Our Lady of the Rock) with its candle-lit interior and hexagonal spire (➤ 58).

- 28C2
- 12km west of Albufeira
- Santola Restaurante, Largo da Fortaleza
  ☎ 082 312332
- Buses from Portimão and Albufeira
- Albufeira (➤ 66)
- Avenida Marginal
  ☎ 282 312145

CALDAS DE MONCHIQUE (➤ 19, TOP TEN)

CARVOEIRO

Carvoeiro is a pretty fishing village which remained virtually untouched until the 1980s, when tourist development began to spread rapidly westwards. Ringed by Moorish-style buildings and the battlemented remains of former fortifications, the sheltered beach can get very crowded at the height of the season, but local fishermen will happily take visitors on trips to the other beaches, such as Benagil and Marinha, and to the nearby caves, tunnels and rock stacks of Algar Seco (➤ 16).

- 28C2
- 16km east of Portimão
- Cafés (£) and seafood restaurants (££) in Estrada do Farol
- Buses from Portimão
- Portimão (➤ 52)
- Praia do Carvoeiro
  ☎ 282 357728

28C2
4km east of Portimão
Cafés (£) around the main square
Buses from Portimão and Albufeira
Portimão (➤ 52)

ESTÔMBAR

Estômbar is a former salt-trading town, with a pretty church, Igreja São Tiago (St James), which is worth a stop for its ornate baroque façade. Typical of the 16th-century Manueline style, its portal is carved with nautical motifs, including stylised shells and ropes in stone. Inside, the columns of the same date are carved with scenes from everyday life. The 18th-century *azulejos* depict St James in combat with the Moors, and the Battle of Lepanto (1571), a famous victory for Christian forces against the might of the Ottoman Turkish navy, as well as more conventional religious scenes.

More appealing to children is the big Slide and Splash aquapark (➤ 110), east of town.

28C2
2km east of Portimão
Cafés (£) along the harbour front
Buses from Portimão and Albufeira
Portimão (➤ 52)

FERRAGUDO

Located on the opposite side of the Arade River estuary from Portimão, Ferragudo is a rare example of an almost untouched coastal fishing village, a reminder of the Algarve as it was less than two decades ago. A timeless atmosphere prevails in the narrow cobbled streets which lead uphill to the simple village church, from whose terrace there are sweeping views over the roof-tops across the boat-filled estuary.

Unspoiled Ferragudo

To the south of the village, the remains of the Castelo de São João de Arade stand on a rocky headland. This medieval fortress, along with the Fortaleza de Santa Catarina on the opposite bank, was built to keep a watch for hostile ships and to prevent them penetrating too far up the river. Now a private house, the fort was turned into a romantic home by the poet Coelho Carvalho at the beginning of the 20th century. From the castle, it is a short stroll to the magnificent Praia Grande. This sandy beach, protected from the open sea by a *molhe* (sea wall), is a good place to learn windsurfing. A short way further south, a lighthouse guides ships up to the main estuary channel.

GUIA

Although Guia has an interesting church, richly decorated with *azulejo* tile pictures, the real attraction here is the Zoomarine Park (► 110) on the edge of this crossroads village. The park combines various attractions: a swimming pool, a pirate castle and a mini-fairground, with a big wheel, a bouncy castle and merry-go-rounds. There are performing dolphins, sealions and parrots, and various animals and marine creatures, including seals, sharks and penguins, are displayed in aquaria and enclosures around the park.

28C2
4km northwest of Albufeira
Cafés (£) around the main square
Buses from Albufeira
Albufeira (► 66)

LAGOA

Lagoa is the Algarve's main wine-producing town, and the local **co-operative**, on the Portimão road, offers guided tours and wine tastings. As well as making both light and full-bodied red wines, the co-operative also produces *aguardente*, a sugar-cane spirit, taken as an aperitif. Another local product worth looking out for is *morgadinhos* – almond-paste sweets in the shape of animals and flowers.

Though no longer the big event it once was, Holy Week is still marked in Lagoa with processions and prayers. The parish church has an 18th-century altar noted for its statue of Nossa Senhora da Luz (Our Lady of Light). Two blocks north, the São José Monastery has a pretty cloister whose garden contains a menhir perhaps dating back to 4000 BC.

28C2
8km east of Portimão
Cafés (£) around the main square
Buses from Portimão and Albufeira
Portimão (► 52)

Adega Co-operativa de Lagoa

N125, Portimão road
282 342181 (in summer book 24 hours in advance)
Daily 9:30–12:30, 2–5:30
Free

Above: azulejo *panel at the monastery of São José*

Traditional irrigation methods inspired this Monchique fountain

MONCHIQUE ✪✪✪

Monchique, the main town in the Serra da Monchique mountain range, attracts summer visitors seeking an escape from the roasting sun of the coastal resorts. Located 458m above sea level, the tree-shaded town usually feels several degrees cooler. Monchique has many natural springs, and the nearby spa village of Caldas de Monchique (➤ 19) is the source of the commercially bottled water sold all over the Algarve. Springs feed the fountain that adorns Monchique's main square, Largo dos Chorões. Cafés, craft shops and art galleries ring the square, offering free tastings of *medronho*, produced by distilling the fermented fruits of the strawberry tree.

Ornate 16th-century carvings decorate the parish church, Nossa Senhora da Conceição, and the gilded altar has many charming details, including angels holding up the sun and the moon. In one of the side chapels, look out for the *azulejos* depicting St Michael in combat with the devil, and the suffering souls in Purgatory.

Many visitors go on to enjoy lunch in one of several restaurants lining the Fóia road that specialise in chilli-flavoured chicken *piri-piri* (➤ 95). You can work up an appetite first by walking to Fóia, the Algarve's highest peak (➤ 59), or following the signposted footpath above the town hall that leads to the ruins of Nossa Senhora do Desterro monastery, a short stroll with fine views.

- 28B3
- 24km north of Portimão
- Cafés in Monchique (£), restaurants on the Monchique to Fóia road
- Buses from Portimão and Silves
- Portimão (➤ 52)
- Largo dos Chorões
  ☎ 282 911189

Handcrafted goods with a Moorish influence in Monchique's craft shops

From Monchique to Caldas de Monchique

This gentle stroll takes you through the attractively wooded countryside surrounding Monchique to the pretty spa town of Caldas de Monchique (➤ 19).

Start in Monchique's main square, Largo dos Chorões. Head south on the main N266 Portimão road.

During spring, you will enjoy the almond-like scent from the mimosa trees that line the roads around Monchique.

After 10 minutes, you will reach the junction between the main Portimão road and the Alferce road, which goes off to the left (east). Take the narrow road between the BP petrol station and the restaurant.

The road now follows the right bank of one of the many small streams that spring up in the Serra da Monchique, eventually flowing down to the sea at Portimão. The road descends through olive groves and orange plantations. To the left you may catch sight of Picota, the Algarve's second highest peak (774m).

After 25 minutes or so, you will cross the Marmelete road. Cross to the continuation of the road on the opposite side. Where it forks, after five minutes, stay on the main road, which bears left. Continue downhill to Caldas de Monchique – the track runs parallel and eventually joins the N266 road on the edge of the town.

As you approach Caldas, look out for the strawberry trees that grow abundantly in the humid environment of the spa town. The fruits of these low-growing evergreen trees are used to produce a fermented liquor which is distilled to make *medronho*. Reward yourself with a glass on completing the walk, but beware – the deceptively smooth taste disguises an alcoholic kick that can be up to 90 per cent proof.

Distance
4km

Time
1½ hours

Start point
Tourist information centre, Largo dos Chorões, Monchique
✚ 28B3

End point
Caldas de Monchique
✚ 28B3

Lunch
Termas de Monchique (£££)
✉ Caldas de Monchique
☎ 282 910910

Almond-scented mimosas in bloom in Monchique's woods

- 28C2
- On the N125 highway, 16km east of Portimão
- Cafés in main square or Porches Velho (££)
- Buses from Portimão and Albufeira
- Carvoeiro (► 47)

Below: *every comfort is provided on this traditional tour boat*

- 28B2
- 18km east of Lagos
- Cafés and restaurants along the quayside
- Railway station 1km to the northwest of the city centre, on Largo Sarrea Prado
- Bus station on Largo do Dique ☎ 282 418120. Buses to Albufeira, Alvor, Armação da Pêra, Faro, Ferragudo, Lagoa, Lagos, Loulé, Monchique, Praia da Rocha, Silves and Torralta
- Avenida Zeca Afonso ☎ 282 419131

PORCHES

Porches is the centre of the Algarve's pottery industry. Though the village is small, there is plenty to see here, as you browse through the displays of terracotta jars and watch artists at work, painting plates and fruit bowls with sunflowers, cockerels or colourful clusters of grapes. Be sure to check whether flower pots and urns are frost proof, otherwise they will shatter if left out over the winter in northern European climes. A trip to Porches can be combined with a visit to The Big One theme park (► 110), between Porches and Alcantarilha.

PORTIMÃO

Portimão is one of the Algarve's main fishing ports, and there is much local life to be enjoyed in and around the city's harbour. The appetising scent of quayside restaurants invites people to come and enjoy a plate of freshly grilled sardines.

If sardines are too humble, you could always take up the challenge of catching your own supper – tuna, perhaps, or hammerhead shark. Fishing trips, for beginners and experienced anglers, are advertised around the quay. Other options include Arade River cruises to Silves, and trips to explore the caves and cliffs at Algar Seco (► 16).

Portimão, with its high-quality shops, is also an excellent place to visit if you prefer real shops to those geared to tourists. Heading inland from the harbour, Rua Dr João Vitorino, Largo 1 de Dezembro and Rua Direita offer plenty of choice. Largo 1 de Dezembro is laid out as a park, with fountains and flower beds, and the benches are decorated with

azulejo pictures depicting key events in Portuguese history. The pictures date from 1924, when Portimão was granted city status by the Portuguese president, Manuel Teixeira Gomes, a native of the town. The adjacent town hall is a fine 18th-century palace, once home to the viscounts of Bívar. The largest church in the Algarve, the Jesuit Igrejo do Colegio, is on the Praça da República.

The 1920s were a prosperous time for Portimão and many of the buildings lining the city centre roads were given decorative tilework façades and pretty wrought-iron balconies, reflecting the art nouveau designs that were then in vogue. The city is currently undergoing redevelopment to create underground parking beneath the main streets, as well as a new marina to the west.

Vast swathes of sand make Praia da Rocha an ever-popular resort

PRAIA DA ROCHA 

Praia da Rocha is one of the most photographed places in the Algarve, with its distinctive, ochre-coloured sandstone columns rising from a broad south-facing beach. This is also one of the Algarve's most hedonistic resorts, popular with young visitors dedicated to making the most of the nightlife on Avenida Tomás Cabreira, the disco- and bar-lined seafront road. At the eastern end of the 2km beach, the Fortaleza de Santa Catarina looks across to Ferragudo's Castelo de São João de Arade. The two fortresses form a 17th-century defensive system designed to guard the Arade River estuary. If you are seeking an escape from the crowds, take a boat trip to the rocky coves at Praia da Vau and Praia dos Três Irmãos.

28B2
2km south of Portimão
Café in the Forteleza (£)
Buses from Portimão
Carvoeiro (► 47)

Food and Drink

Algarvian cooking has absorbed Spanish, Moorish and African influences, but nothing epitomises the region better than the simple charcoal-grilled sardine, savoured out of doors at a seafront café on a balmy summer's evening.

Amêijoas na cataplana, *a traditional seafood dish*

Algarvian Dishes

The region's cuisine reflects the ready availability of all kinds of fresh fish, from eels, lampreys and swordfish to lobsters, whelks, limpets and barnacles. Lobster, sea bass, mullet and bream are costed according to their weight and seasonal price (*preço variavel*) – check before you order to prevent an unexpectedly expensive meal. Most fish are simply grilled over a charcoal brazier, to seal in the fresh flavours, but tuna is more often baked with a sauce of peppers and tomatoes, and stuffed with a mixture of sausage, bacon, tomatoes and rice.

Shellfish features in two of the region's most typical specialities: *amêijoas na cataplana* and *arroz de marisco.* The latter is the Algarvian version of paella, a rich, slightly liquid mixture of clams, prawns and fish, cooked with rice, onions, tomatoes and peppers. *Cataplana*, named after the copper vessel in which it is cooked, is a delicious stew of clams, sausage, ham, onions, garlic, chilli and herbs. The

Spanish-influenced arroz de marisco *(spicy seafood rice)*

tightly clamped *cataplana* seals all the flavour in, to be released in a cloud of fragrant steam when the dish is ceremonially opened at your table. Some restaurants offer up to a dozen different *cataplana* variations, using combinations of pork, chicken, lobster, monkfish, shellfish and prawns.

Portuguese Dishes

You will also find dishes from other parts of Portugal on the menu, including *caldeirada* (fish soup), based on stock made from the heads and bones of locally caught fish, enriched with paprika, onions, tomatoes and potatoes. *Bacalhau à brás* is fried salted cod with potatoes, onions, garlic, olives and eggs. The ubiquitous *caldo verde* (green soup) is a popular starter, made from potatoes, onions and finely shredded cabbage, with spicy *chouriço* sausage for added piquancy.

The perfect snack – cakes made from egg yolks and soft cheese

Inland Cuisine

Though fish is also popular inland, you will find dishes on rural restaurant menus that rarely feature on the coast. Pigs' trotters with beans and black pudding, or liver and rice, may not be to everyone's taste, but few can resist the spicy taste of chicken *piri-piri* (flavoured with chilli oil), a speciality of the Monchique region, or *caldeirada de cabrito*, a casserole of lamb or kid with onions, tomatoes and potatoes. Game (wild boar, quail, partridge and pheasant) features in season, and if nothing else appeals, try delicious *bife à Portuguesa* – grilled sirloin steak.

Fine port is a favourite after-dinner indulgence

Wine

Although the Algarve has its own wines, they lack the finesse of nobler ones from the north of Portugal. Try white port (*porto branco*) served chilled as an aperitif, rather than post-prandial red. *Dão* and the similar *Barraida* are good all-purpose wines: both red and white versions are aged in barrels to acquire an oaky flavour, but the best remain soft and fruity. In hot weather, try something lighter – such as semi-sparkling *vinho verde* (green wine – so called due to its youthfulness rather than its colour), with a palate-cleansing lemon tang.

28C2
21km north of Albufeira
Café (£) near the church
Buses from Silves
Silves (► 44)

SÃO BARTOLOMEU DE MESSINES

São Bartolomeu is a typical inland town in the fertile foothills of the Serra do Caldeirão mountains, where almonds, carob, figs and pomegranates alternate with fields of wheat or vegetables. Rua Remexido is one of several streets lined by the characteristic Algarvian houses, with whitewashed walls and the door and window frames picked out in vibrant reds and blues. The street is named after the guerrilla leader who lived here for several years and who controlled much of the western Algarve in the 1830s, during the civil war between right-wing supporters of King Miguel I, and liberal supporters of his brother and predecessor, the late King Pedro IV.

The parish church, Igreja Matriz, is a fine building in a mixture of styles, with a baroque façade, an elegant stone pulpit carved from local granite, and chapels decorated with 17th-century tiles and 16th- to 18th-century statues.

Some 10km west of the town is the Barragem de Arade, a reservoir created by damming the River Arade, a popular resort for anglers, with watersports facilities and several cafés along its shores.

Almonds feature in folklore and also in many sweet confections

Did you know ?

Legend has it that the almonds which grow in such abundance in the western Algarve were introduced to the region by a Moorish emir whose homesick Scandinavian wife longed to see the snow. The trees flower between late December and the end of February, and the wilted blossoms resemble snow as they drift from the trees, stirred by the breezes of early spring.

Portimão to Monchique

This splendid half-day drive takes in the historic town of Silves and the mountain scenery of the Serra de Monchique, but it can be extended to a whole day.

From Portimão, cross the River Arade using the old bridge and follow the minor road to Lagoa.

Church lovers will want to stop in Estômbar (➤ 48) for the Manueline portal and *azulejos*, and in Lagoa (➤ 49) for the São José Monastery, with its pretty cloister.

From Lagoa, head north on the N124 to Silves, passing under the new motorway.

Approaching Silves from the south gives a fine view of the walled hilltown and its castle. Park by the river and climb up to the castle, cathedral and archaeological museum (➤ 44).

Leave Silves on the road to São Bartolomeu de Messines, stopping to look at the Cruz de Portugal beside the roundabout as you exit the town's suburbs. After 5km, turn left for a view of the Barragem de Arade reservoir. Follow the minor road that leads, via Amorosa, to São Bartolomeu, and join the IP1 (also signposted the N264/E01) to Lisbon. Leave at the next exit, after 15km, signposted to São Marcos da Serra and Nave Redonda. Cross the railway line west of the IP1 to find signs to Monchique.

Many distractions may tempt you to stop – you could take a closer look at the cork oak trees to see how the bark is stripped, or perhaps enjoy the wayside wild flowers.

At Nave Redonda, in the Alentejo, turn south to return to the Algarve along a scenic road that climbs to Monchique (➤ 50).

You can extend the tour by climbing Fóia, the Algarve's highest peak (➤ 59), or choose a restaurant (➤ 95) and enjoy lunch with views.

Head south to Caldas de Monchique (➤ 19) and stroll around the flower-filled streets. To return to Portimão, continue south on the N266.

Distance
110km

Time
6 hours

Start/end point
Portimão
28B2

Lunch
Paraíso da Montanha (££)
Estrada da Fóia, Monchique
282 912150

Born in Lisbon, St Anthony is celebrated in many churches

28C3
22km north of Portimão
Cafés and restaurants in Monchique and on the Fóia road (➤ 95)
Aljezur (➤ 35)

Rounded hills clothed in woods typify the Serra de Monchique

SERRA DE MONCHIQUE 

The Serra de Monchique range forms a distinctive group of hills in the western Algarve. Running from west to east, the hills act as a barrier to cold air from the land mass to the north, helping to maintain the balmy warmth of the Algarvian winter. The woodlands are a mixture of cork oak, sweet chestnut and arbutus, with the addition of pine, eucalyptus, mimosa and great plane. The hills are volcanic in origin and the igneous rocks are quarried around the village of Nave, lying between Monchique (➤ 50) and the spa town of Caldas de Monchique (➤ 19).

From Nave, the N267 road cuts westward though the hills to Aljezur (➤ 35). Forest fires have scarred part of the route, but this delightful road passes mainly through leafy woodland, past hillsides cut into terraces for vegetable cultivation, and fast-flowing streams. On the way, Caseis is worth a stop for its medieval church and the nearby ruins of what is claimed to be a Roman fort.

28C2
4km west of Armação da Pêra
Café (£) at Cova Redonda, many more in Armação de Pêra
Armação de Pêra (➤ 47)

VILA SENHORA DA ROCHA 

The sparkling white chapel that stands on the cliff edge at Vila Senhora da Rocha dates from at least the 13th century – a worn capital in the triple-arched entrance porch is Visigothic in origin, dating back to the 6th century. The chapel has long been a place of pilgrimage for devout Portuguese who come here to pray to the Virgin in this idyllic spot. Below the chapel are the quiet beaches of Praia Nova and Praia Senhora da Rocha. Fishermen provide a casual ferry service from here to several other isolated beaches, at Albandeira, Barranquinho, Marinha and Benagil.

Scaling the Algarve's Highest Peak

This hike through the wooded hills west of Monchique takes you to the top of 902m Fóia, the highest peak in the Algarve. Begin early in the morning for the coolest walking conditions.

Distance
16km

Time
5 hours

Start/end point
Tourist information centre, Largo dos Chorões, Monchique
28B3

Lunch
Quinta de São Bento (£££)
Estrada da Fóia, Monchique
282 912143

Start in Monchique's main square, Largo dos Chorões. Take Rua Porto Funda (the top right-hand exit) and then turn left up to Rua do Castelo. Turn right to reach the N501 road, signposted to Barranco dos Pisões and Foz de Farelo. Follow the road for 1km, and take the track left, signposted Portela das Eiras. Climb up to the village on the broad track. At the crossroads in the village, turn right, then immediately left along a path that climbs through a cultivated valley, with the stream on your right. Bear right uphill, through eucalyptus woodland. After bending to the left and then left again, the path descends for a short distance, before climbing for the final ascent on a rocky path up to the summit.

Impressive views from the lofty summit of Fóia

Be guided by the cluster of TV masts that crowd the summit of Fóia. These will not spoil the fine views from the *miradouro* (viewpoint) on the mountain top, which stretch to the Atlantic in the west, the Barragem de Arade reservoir to the south and the rolling hills of the Alentejo to the north. There is a shop and café at the summit.

The easiest way back to Monchique is down the tarmac Estrada da Fóia road, the N265. Alternatively, look out for the track that heads almost due south from the miradouro, *following a river valley to join the N265 road, cutting out a 2km loop in the road. Another option is to take the N265 road for 300m and then the track to the right that descends via Cruz da Fóia and Cascalho dos Erades back to Portela das Eiras.*

AL 33 L
AL 55 L
MARIA HELENA

Eastern Central Algarve

Between Albufeira (west) and Faro (east) lie most of the Algarve's big holiday resorts – Vilamoura, Quarteira, Vale do Lobo, Quinta do Lago and Albufeira itself – tempting visitors with their white-washed villas set around manicured lawns, and miles of sandy beaches stretching to the horizon. Yet, unless you are staying in one of these resorts, you need never know of their existence: most lie to the south of the main road system, built on poor sandy soils on the marshy fringes of the Algarvian coast. If the fishermen have seen their coast transformed, the rich and fertile inland region has scarcely been changed by tourism at all, and prosperous cities – including the Algarvian capital, Faro, and the second city, Loulé – offer the chance to flow with the mainstream of everyday Portuguese life.

'Five leagues to Faro thro a beautiful countryside. On the one hand the sea, on the other mountains. It is rich, yet not wholly cultivated. The occasional odour of orange gardens was like Mohammed's paradise.'

ROBERT SOUTHEY
Visiting the Algarve (1801)

Colourful confusion – Albufeira's popular beach is also home to the local fishing fleet

Faro

29D1
Railway station is on Avenida da República, at the northern end
Bus terminus is in Avenida da República, by the port ☎ 289 899760, with services to and from Albufeira, Armação de Pêra, Estói, Lagoa, Loulé, Monte Gordo, Olhão, Portimão, Quarteira, São Brás de Alportel, Tavira, Vilamoura, Vila Real de Santo António
Olhão (► 86)
Rua da Misericórdia 8–12 ☎ 289 803604

Visitors arriving at Faro airport could be forgiven for judging the Algarvian capital to be a dusty industrial town with nothing to offer. So it looks from the airport road, with its heavy traffic and jumble of seemingly unplanned tower blocks and light-industrial estates. Yet, at the centre of all this chaos, there is a quiet walled city of immense historic character, as well as a lively shopping centre, where cosmopolitan Faroites meet for lunch in the outdoor cafés of the traffic-free streets, or stroll after work in the cool of the evening.

The port is the best area from where to begin a tour of the city. The 18th-century Alfândega (Customs House), with its elegant wrought-iron balcony, is to the north of the port basin, overlooking an obelisk commemorating Ferreira d'Almeida (1847–1910), former naval minister and citizen of Faro. From the adjacent Jardim Manuel Bivar public gardens it is a short step to the impressive Arco da Vila (Town Gate, with the tourist information centre alongside). This imposing baroque archway, with its stork's nest and statue of St Thomas Aquinas, Faro's patron saint, serves as a stately entrance to the calm streets of the old walled city.

The 13th-century wall that protects the old city was solid enough to survive the 1755 earthquake, but the handsome stone palaces that line the streets, and the beautiful

Ancient and modern buildings ring Faro's sheltered harbour

convent buildings of the main square, all date from the latter end of the 18th century. There is a great contrast between the huge cathedral and magnificent bishop's palace, and the more domestic streets to the south and east of the walled city, with their wrought-iron balconies and peeling façades draped with washing.

Did you know ?

In 1596, the Earl of Essex sacked the city of Faro (then under Spanish administration) as part of a plan to forestall the departure of the Spanish Armada. The city was burned to the ground, but Essex rescued some 200 leather-bound volumes, which formed the library of the scholarly Bishop Ossorio. Two years later, Essex donated the books to the Bodleian, the new library in Oxford founded by his friend, Sir Thomas Bodley.

One or two of those nearest to the Arco do Repouso have been converted to chic shops and restaurants. Near by is a statue of King Afonso III, who in 1249 captured the city from the Moors and expelled them from the Algarve. He is said to have rested here after vanquishing the Moors, hence the name of the gate – the Arco do Repouso (Arch of Repose).

From the intimacy of the walled city, the arch leads out to the huge Largo de São Francisco, a square that is used for carnivals and feast days. Crossing the square, it is a short walk up Rua do Bocage and left into Rua de Portugal to the regional museum, and from there to Rua de Santo António, the shop- and café-lined pedestrian street that leads back to the harbour.

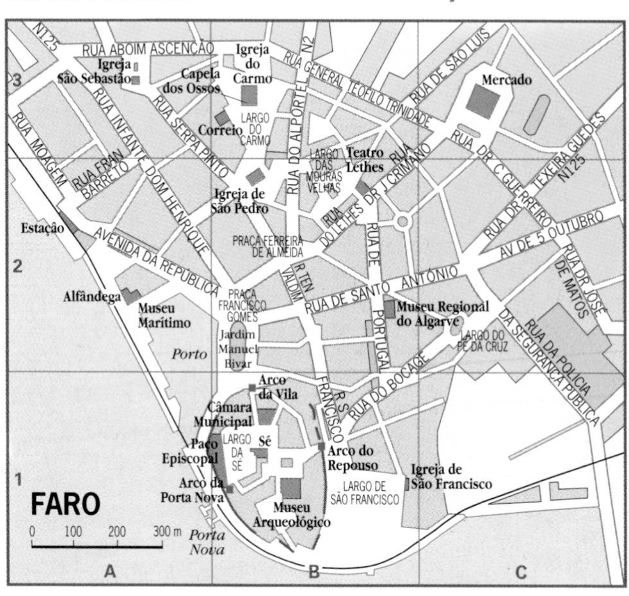

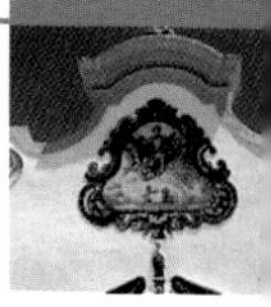

What to See in Faro

IGREJA DO CARMO (► 20, TOP TEN)

MUSEU ARQUEOLÓGICO 

Faro's archaeological museum is housed in the Convento da Nossa Senhora da Assunção, whose elegant 16th-century, two-storey cloister survived the earthquake of 1755. The ground floor's archaeological collection includes Roman and medieval funerary monuments, Manueline window frames, a Moorish stele inscribed with Arabic characters, and finds from the Roman villa at Milreu (► 24). Upstairs the miscellaneous collection includes everything from dress uniforms and heavy Sino-Portuguese rosewood furniture, to art nouveau vases and kitsch ashtrays.

- 63B1
- Largo Dom Afonso III
- 289 824085
- Nov–Mar Mon, Sat 2:30–6, Tue–Fri 9:30–5:30; Apr–Oct Mon, Sat 2:30–6, Tue–Fri 10–6
- Few
- Moderate

MUSEU MARÍTIMO 

Housed in the same building as the harbour authority, this museum contains model ships – from 15th-century caravels to modern naval gunships, as well as a collection of colourful shells and models explaining the techniques of the fishing industry. In contrast with today's high-tech factory ships, with sonar devices and sweep nets, the sardine and tuna boats shown here seem charmingly antiquated.

- 63A2
- 289 803601
- Capitania do Porto de Faro
- Mon–Fri 2:30–4:30
- Few
- Moderate

MUSEU REGIONAL DO ALGARVE 

The grainy pictures and displays of saddlery, straw-weaving, salt-panning, net-weaving and lace-making in this museum give a picture of everyday life in the Algarve as it was until the mid 1970s, and still remains in the more remote rural regions. Among the museum's fascinating exhibits are reconstructions of typical village interiors and displays of ornamented chimneypots.

- 63B2
- 289 827610
- Rua do Pé da Cruz
- Mon–Fri 9:30–12:30, 2:30–5:30. Closed Sat, Sun and public hols
- Few
- Moderate

SÉ (CATHEDRAL) 

Faro's cathedral is a fine example of both change and continuity, standing on the site of the main mosque of the Moorish city, which itself replaced the remains of a Visigothic church built on the ruins of the Roman basilica. The 1755 earthquake demolished much of the original 13th-century cathedral, leaving only the truncated stump of the tower. The interior can be deliciously cool on a hot summer day. The Gothic chapel on the south side, with its rib vaults and bosses, survives from the 15th century, and the rest is typically 18th century, with gorgeous gilded woodwork and blue *azulejos*.

- 63B1
- Largo da Sé
- Mon–Fri 10–12, 2–5. Closed Sat, Sun and public hols
- Few
- Moderate

Left: *calm cloisters house Faro's art collections*

What to See in Eastern Central Algarve

ALBUFEIRA

28C2
36km west of Faro
Cafés (£) in Rua 5 de Outubro; O Penedo (££) in Rua Latino Coelho 15
Buses from Faro
Rua 5 de Outubro
289 585279
Loulé (➤ 68)

Albufeira typifies the way that tourism has transformed the sleepy fishing towns of the Algarvian coast into today's bustling holiday resorts. Until the 1960s, only fishermen used the beach below the town. They still do, bringing in their daily catch every morning, but now they are surrounded by thousands of sun-bronzed bodies.

The narrow cobbled streets of the old fishing village above now play host to boutiques, bars and restaurants, and the beach is reached by a tunnel. Albufeira has grown so big that it takes in several adjacent bays, and a more modern centre of tourism has grown up on Avenida Dr Francisco Carveiro, 2km to the east, also known as 'the Strip'. Here you will find a plethora of English-style pubs and discos. The streets are paved with black and white mosaics, a traditional form of paving that was originally invented as a way of using up the rubble from houses demolished by the 1755 earthquake.

To the west of the old town a new marina is taking shape, due to be completed in 2003.

From old Albufeira you can walk to Baleeira along the cliffs, passing the Xorino cave, where the Moors took refuge when Albufeira was reconquered by the Christians in the 13th century. At Praia de Galé, 8km to the west, the beaches offer windsurfing and scuba diving.

Cobbled café-lined streets in the holiday paradise of Albufeira

ALMANCIL ✪✪✪

Almancil has little traditional character but has grown rapidly in recent years, becoming a service centre for the upmarket resorts at Vale do Lobo and Quinta do Lago, and boasting some of the best interior design galleries, shops and restaurants along the Algarve. One outstanding attraction draws visitors here – the church of São Lourenço dos Matos (St Lawrence of the Woods), beside the main N125 road east of the town (just before the start of the Almancil bypass). The interior of this domed, whitewashed church is covered in blue and white *azulejos*, dating from 1730. The side walls have six scenes from the saint's life. The gilded altarpiece, typical of those found on the Algarve, is known as *talha dourada*. Just below the church, the **Centro Cultural São Lourenço** displays modern art and hosts jazz and contemporary music concerts.

29D2
13km northwest of Faro
Church open daily 9–1 and 2:30–6
Café (£) in Centro Cultural
Moderate
Vale do Lobo (➤ 74)

Centro Cultural São Lourenço
289 395475
Tue–Sun 10–7

ALTE (➤ 17, TOP TEN)

THE BARROCAL ✪✪✪

The Barrocal stretches from São Brás de Alportel in the east, across to Silves in the west, down to the N125 highway in the south and up to the Serra do Caldeirão hills in the north. Despite its stony appearance, this region is highly fertile, with deep, rich soils derived from eroded limestone. For centuries, local farmers have been clearing the boulders to create fields bounded by the massive drystone walls that are such a feature of the region. These walls, and the bare fields – known as *terra rossa* (red earth) – are rust red in colour, reflecting the large amounts of iron in the soil. Once cleared, the fields are ploughed and planted with oranges, almonds, figs, carobs (for animal fodder) and vines.

28C2/29D2
Cafés in Alte and Loulé
Loulé (➤ 68)

The Barrocal is sparsely populated and villages are tranquil and unhurried. Wildlife flourishes; in spring or early summer, you will not have to look far to see bulbs and rare orchids in flower, and at night you will hear the sound of owls, bats and foxes.

Empty landscapes in the Barrocal provide a refuge for wildlife

To visit the Barrocal, take the road from Alte to Benafim Grande, then head south via Alto Fica, following signs for Loulé, or the road that runs further east, from Salir to Loulé and on to São Brás de Alportel.

29D2
12km northeast of Albufeira
Cafés (£) in the main street
Loulé (➤ below)

BOLIQUEIME

This small settlement, 1km north of the N125, seems almost bypassed by modern tourism. The few visitors who stop here now do so because of the novels of Lídia Jorge, one of Portugal's best-known modern writers, born here in 1946. One of her most popular novels, *The Day of the Miracle* (1982), is set in a fictional Algarvian village called Vilamaninhos, loosely based on Boliqueime.

ESTÓI (➤ 22, TOP TEN)

29D2
Bus terminus is in Rua Nossa Senhora de Fátima
289 416655, with services to and from Albufeira, Almancil, Alte, Armação de Pêra, Faro, Lagoa, Messines, Portimão and Quarteira
Alte (➤ 17)
Edifício do Castelo, Rua de Paio Peres Correia 17
289 463900

LOULÉ

Loulé is a city to savour at leisure, arriving early in the day for the market and exploring the attractive streets and historic buildings before lunch. The second most populous city in the Algarve, it combines bustling modernity – symbolised by the space-age church prominently sited on the hilltop to the west of the city – with narrow, cobbled alleys where saddlers, metal workers and seamstresses carry on age-old craft traditions.

Parking can be a problem, but spaces are often available around Largo de São Francisco. From here, pedestrianised Rua de 5 Outubro leads to Largo Dr Bernardo Lopes, at the foot of Praça da República, the city's main street. The first right turn (Rua de Paio Peres Correia) takes you to the **Museu Municipal** (Municipal Museum) and tourist office, which are built against the few remaining walls of the town's medieval castle. The museum displays flint tools and pottery fragments from the many prehistoric grave sites in the area, as well as a number of Iron-Age stele (incised grave markers).

Opposite (on the corner with Rua Vice-Almirante Cândido dos Reis) is the delightful Espirito Santo

Space-age Nossa Senhora da Piedade on a hill above Loulé

monastery, with its quiet, shady cloister. Part of the monastery has been turned into a Municipal Art Gallery, with changing exhibitions by contemporary artists. Heading downhill from here, cobbled Rua das Bicas Velhas ('The Street of the Old Spouts') is named after the spring-fed drinking fountains, set below a coat of arms, at the bottom of the street.

To the right of here, Praça Dom Alfonso III takes you outside the ancient city walls for a view back up to the surviving medieval towers, then the modern Rua da Mouraria follows the line of the ancient walls for a short distance until you find the steep alley called Calçada dos Sapateiros (Shoemakers' Alley).

The narrow alley opens out into the square that is dominated by Loulé's Gothic parish church, **São Clemente**. The tower survives from the 12th century, originally built as the minaret, or prayer tower, of the city's Moorish mosque. Though now hung with bells, and given a short dome and steeple, the minaret is one of the few examples of Arabic architecture to survive in the Algarve. Inside are several splendid side chapels – notably the 16th-century São Brás chapel and the São Crispim chapel. To the west of the church is the palm-shaded Jardim dos Amuados, the enigmatically named 'Sulky People's Garden'. In the opposite direction, Rua Martim Farto leads to the Municipal Market, a vast Moorish-style building that covers a whole block in the city centre. Both within the market and in the surrounding streets there are shops and stalls selling everything from animal feed and (sadly) caged songbirds to cheese, dried herbs, olives, honey and fruit.

From the colourful market, with its façade decorated with art nouveau tiles, Praça da República runs downhill, back to Rua 5 de Outubro, lined with many cafés.

From mosque minaret to Christian belfry at São Clemente church

Museu Municipal
✉ Rua de Paio Peres Correia 17
☎ 289 415000 (ext. 211)
🕐 Mon–Fri 9–5:30, Sat 10–2
♿ Few
✋ Free

São Clemente
✉ Largo Batalão dos Sapadores do Caminho
🕐 Daily 10–1, 2–7
♿ Few
✋ Free

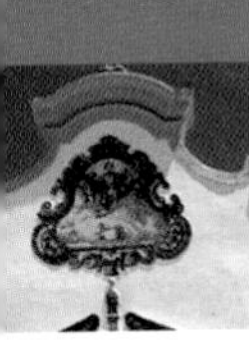

MILREU (➤ 24, TOP TEN)

PADERNE ✪✪

29D2
12km north of Albufeira
Castle open 24 hours
Cafés (£) near the parish church
Loulé (➤ 68)

Paderne is an attractive village on the western edge of the Barrocal. High-walled villas with beautiful gardens in the hills to the east indicate that this is a favourite retreat for wealthy Algarvians. For visitors, it is not the village that is of interest so much as the castle on its outskirts.

The castle is well signposted from Paderne. You can either drive all the way, or walk the last two kilometres.

Drive through the village northwards (downhill), and turn left at the right-angled bend at the bottom of the main street. As you exit the town, look for another left turn (signposted '*Fontes*'). This becomes a rough track after a short distance, passing through cultivated fields. The track leads to a commercial water bottling plant, where spring water gushes from spouts into a large, stone trough.

Turn left at the plant, then immediately right and follow the red earth track that winds through fields. At the next junction, turn left and follow the track up to the castle.

If you would rather walk the last stretch, turn right at the junction and continue until the track ends by the river. Park and enjoy the view across the Ribeira de Quarteira to the water mill on the other side. At this point a track leads straight on along the river bank. If you walk along it for 1km, you will reach a 16th-century packhorse bridge with its grinding stones lying among the weed-covered walls. Beside the bridge, a steep path climbs up to the right and leads, after another 1km, to Paderne Castle. There is a more direct route to the castle from the riverside car park – straight up the hill via any of the steep sheep tracks.

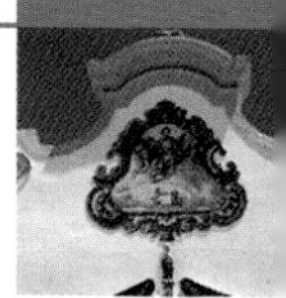

Spring in Paderne brings blue skies and clouds of blossom

The castle's external walls survive to a good height, but it is not possible to explore the interior of the castle. Rubble fills the chapel that was built after the castle was conquered in 1249 in a fierce and bloody battle between the Moors and the Christian army of King Afonso III.

The ambience of the site is somewhat spoilt by traffic noise, but you'll have panoramic views of the countryside.

QUARTEIRA ✪

One of the first Algarvian resorts to be developed, Quarteira's utilitarian hotel blocks are a million miles away in spirit from the villas of later resorts, which mirror traditional Algarvian architecture in scale and colouring.

Despite its lack of charm, however, the town has a long sandy beach and a seafront promenade lined with seafood restaurants and bars. In the old quarter, there is a lively fish and produce market, and the gypsy market, held on Wednesdays, is one of the best and biggest in the region. Just north of the resort is the big Atlantic Park pool and waterslide complex (➤ 110).

- 29D2
- 11km southwest of Loulé
- Cafés (£) on Rua Abertura Mar; Sea Horse, Dutch Pancake House (£) on Avenida Infante de Sagres
- Bus station on Avenida Sá Carneiro ☎ 289 389143 with services to and from Albufeira, Loulé and Vilamoura
- Loulé (➤ 68)

QUERENÇA ✪

A modest, but atmospheric, farming village in the Barrocal region, Querença is a good spot to enjoy a leisurely lunch, with two well-regarded restaurants on the main square. Choose between pavement tables with views of the pretty, onion-domed tower of the parish church, or interior views stretching for miles over the Barrocal countryside. As well as its carved and gilded baroque altar surrounds, the parish church has a small collection of painted wood statues dating from the 16th and 17th centuries.

- 29D2
- 9km north of Loulé
- Restaurante de Querença (££, ➤ 97)
- Loulé (➤ 68)

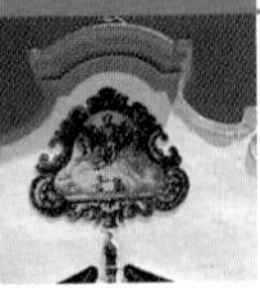

ROCHA DA PENA

29D2
9km east of Alte, 17km northwest of Loulé
Café das Grutas (£)
Alte (➤ 17)

The cliff-like Rocha da Pena is a wall of limestone rising to a height of 479m in the north of the Barrocal (➤ 67). To walk to the rock, take the well-defined path signposted right of the Café de Grutas, in the tiny settlement of Rocha. (Rocha is reached by car along a dirt road left off the Penina/Pena road, just outside Penina).

The path climbs through typical scrub, with low-growing holy oak, cistus and dwarf fan-palm. The walk takes around 40 minutes, and once you reach the summit (marked by a trig point), you will be rewarded with fine views.

On Salir's ruined castle ramparts, only a few massive stone blocks remain

SALIR

29D2
14km north of Loulé
Café Moura, Rua dos Muros do Castelo
Loulé (➤ 68)

Salir's huge 12th-century castle survives in the form of a cobbled rampart walk, which passes some huge bastions of concreted rubble, all that remains after villagers robbed the walls of their facing masonry in the past. From the western stretch of the ramparts, there is a good view over the hillside olive groves and the patchwork of cultivated fields in the valley below to the Rocha da Pena, which marks the northern edge of the Barrocal region (➤ 67).

The castle is one of the few Moorish structures to survive in the Algarve, and its scale is illustrated by the number of more recent houses that now fill the interior. Though heavily defended, the castle fell to Christian forces in 1249, towards the end of the campaign to drive the Moors from Portugal. The parish church occupies a high platform (shared with a huge water tower) with fine views over the Barrocal countryside. Inside, there is an unusual Last Judgement scene on the north wall.

Fonte de Benémola

On this walk you will see typical Barrocal vegetation, as well as wildflowers, butterflies and grasshoppers. Take a torch with you if you want to explore the nearby caves.

To reach the start of the walk, follow the N396 north out of Loulé, turn left after 9km (signposted Querença) but ignore the Querença turning at the next junction, continuing on the main road for 2km until the brown Fonte de Benémola signpost on the right (just beyond the village of Vale Mulher). Turn off here and park at the side of the dirt track that leads to the spring (it is not an official car park but there is room for around 10 cars). The broad track to the Fonte passes between drystone walls, and there are red and white paint splashes on the wall to indicate the correct route every time the track divides. After walking for around 1km, cross a bridge and turn left.

It is another 1km or so to the first spring and there is an even more delightful spot 200m further up the track, with a rocky ford and a mossy pool. Wild flowers, along with butterflies and grasshoppers, thrive in the damp atmosphere of the reedy river margins and on the limestone screes around. On the escarpment above the springs are two caves, reached by continuing along the boulder-strewn track, then turning right to climb uphill on a well-defined path.

At the next junction, take the right-hand track (not the one that continues uphill) and the caves are reached after 100m and 150m respectively.

It is impossible to penetrate the caves very far without a torch, but you can stand at the entrance and imagine what life might have been like as a prehistoric cave dweller.

Take the same route in reverse to return to the main road.

Distance
5km

Time
2 hours

Start/end point
Roadside car park, 2km west of Querença
28D2

Lunch
Restaurante de Querença (££)
Largo da Igreja, Querença
289 422540

Catching sight of bright butterflies is one of the tour's many pleasures

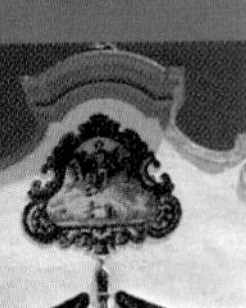

VALE DO LOBO

29D1
12km south of Loulé
Several bars and restaurants (£–£££) in Rua da República; good restaurants (££–£££) on the road between Vale do Lobo and Almancil
Loulé (► 68)

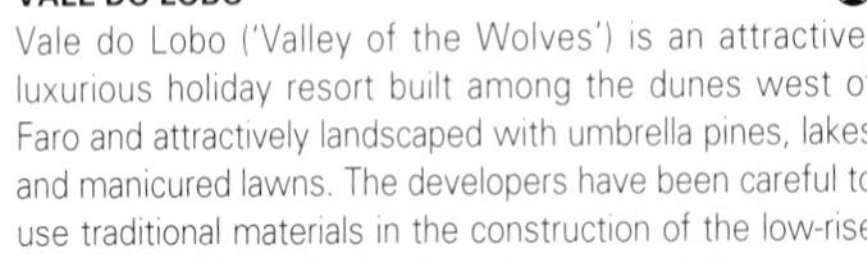

Vale do Lobo ('Valley of the Wolves') is an attractive, luxurious holiday resort built among the dunes west of Faro and attractively landscaped with umbrella pines, lakes and manicured lawns. The developers have been careful to use traditional materials in the construction of the low-rise villas with whitewashed walls and orange roof tiles.

The sandy beaches of Vale do Lobo and nearby Vale do Garrão (also known as Paradise Beach) are lined with bars and fish restaurants, and there are watersports facilities here and at neighbouring Quinta do Lago. A great part of Vale do Lobo's appeal, however, is its proximity to the some outstanding golf courses (► 115). There are plenty of organisations offering cycling, horse riding and walking trips into the adjacent Ria Formosa Nature Reserve (► 26).

VILAMOURA

29D2
11km southwest of Loulé
Restaurants (£–£££) around the marina
From Faro and Quarteira

Cerro da Vila
Avenida Cerro da Vila
289 312153
9–12:30, 2–6
Moderate

The purpose-built resort of Vilamoura has, as its focal point, a large marina ringed by shops, bars and restaurants. From here it is a short walk to the sandy beach, and there are further beaches near by at Falésia. The region benefits from excellent golf courses, tennis centres, fitness centres, horse-riding schools and watersports facilities, all within walking distance. Though the current resort dates back only to the 1970s, the site has a surprisingly interesting history. The **Cerro da Vila Museu e Estação Arqueológica**, north of the waterfront, is a new archaeological park created at the site of a Roman settlement and later Moorish farm. Remains include the floor plan of a Roman villa, complete with bathhouse.

Pastel-painted holiday homes line the seafront at Vilamoura

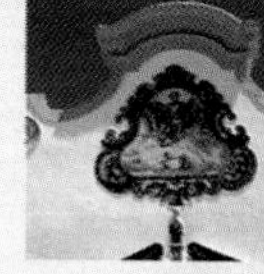

Central Highlights

This drive takes in farming hamlets, green river valleys, gnarled olive trees and scented orange groves. Consider stopping for a leisurely lunch in Alte or Querença.

From Loulé, head out west on the N270 road signposted to Boliqueime (➤ 68).

As you leave the town, a wide new road to the left leads up to the unusual modern church of Nossa Senhora da Piedade. It is worth driving up for the views from the terrace in front of the church and for the little 16th-century chapel alongside.

Continue to Boliqueime and take the road north (signed Lisbon) to Paderne (➤ 70).

Wild woodland and olive groves give the Barrocal its distinctive feel

Take the road north out of the town and divert left to explore the well-preserved 12th-century castle above the River Quarteira.

Drive on through the village of Purgatório, continue to Portela de Messines, then turn right for Alte.

Alte (➤ 17) is the Algarve's most attractive village. The church was built in the 13th century by the local overlord as a thank-offering for his safe return from the Crusades, and has some fine statuary and tile work. The river tumbles through the village, over a mini waterfall and past converted mill buildings. Continue eastwards, stopping to scale Rocha da Pena, if time allows, or to explore Salir castle (➤ 72).

From Salir take the minor road south to Vicentes, and turn left. After 2km, the road crosses a bridge, turns sharp left in front of a mill, and then sharp right. A short way on, on the right, is the start of the Fonte de Benémola walk (➤ 73). Continue on to Querença, then to the main road and turn right to return to Loulé.

Distance
74km

Time
7 hours

Start/end point
Loulé
29D2

Lunch
Alte Hotel (££)
Montino, Alte (signposted on the road to Santa Margerida, 1km northwest of the town)
289 478523

Eastern Algarve

Robert Southey's description of the Eastern Algarve (below) remains as accurate today as at the beginning of the 19th century. Away from the coast, the countryside consists of a great, rolling succession of hills, covered in wild Mediterranean scrub, interspersed with cork oak trees. Southey found it monotonous, but modern travellers will probably revel in the sight of so much unspoiled countryside. In the future, dense forests will make this landscape look very different.

The homogeneity of the central hilly region contrasts with the pleasing variety of the region's coastal and riverine scenery. The broad, flat valley of the River Guadiana, with its bird-filled shores and reed beds, is endlessly fascinating, and the town of Vila Real offers a gateway to the very different Spanish region of Andalucia. The coastal towns include the port of Olhão, the city of Tavira and the resort of Monte Gordo, with its glorious beach and holiday atmosphere.

*'It is a strange country…
mountain all round
swelling, breasting,
surging like a sea.'*

ROBERT SOUTHEY
Visiting the Algarve (1801)

Looking across the River Guadiana from Alcoutim to Spanish Sanlúcar

Tavira

This distinctive town has a greater variety of architectural detail than most. Both banks of the River Gilão, which passes through the centre, are lined by noble houses with baroque window frames and balustraded parapets. Most have wrought-iron balconies, whose decoration is mirrored in the railings of the pedestrian bridge that links the two sides of the town. The hip-gabled roofs are highly distinctive, known as *tesouro* (treasure) roofs.

29E2

Railway station is on Rua da Liberdade

Bus terminus is in Rua dos Pelames ☎ 281 322546, with services to and from Cabanas, Cacela, Faro, Monte Gordo, Olhão, Pedras d'El Rei, Santa Luzia and Vila Real de Santo António

Olhão (➤ 86)

Rua da Galeria ☎ 281 322511

Wealth from the Portuguese colonies was lavished on Tavira's numerous churches, whose turrets and belfries add further interest to the skyline. The best place to view all this architectural diversity is from the walls of the castle (➤ opposite) on the south bank of the river. Cross the footbridge, take the first turn right, climbing uphill, past the tourist office, and pause to admire the superb Renaissance doorcase to the Church of Nossa Senhora da Misericórdia (Our Lady of Mercy). Above the portal, angels hold aside curtains to reveal the figure of the praying Virgin. Turning

Wrought-iron railings mirror the elegant balconies of Tavira

left takes you to the castle, and to the hilltop church of Santa Maria do Castelo (➤ below).

Heading north from the castle, turn down Rua Detraz dos Muros to Rua dos Pelames; this riverside street has some rare 16th-century houses, distinguished by stone doorcases which survived the 1755 earthquake. Crossing the footbridge again takes you down Rua 5 de Outubro to São Paulo church (➤ below). Restaurants and bars line the square in front of the church (Praça Dr Padinha), and the streets running to the south and east. Look out for the latticed doors, made of turned and woven strips of wood.

Beach huts offer shade and shelter on the Ilha de Tavira

What to See in Tavira

CASTELO

Tavira's Moorish castle was rebuilt after the Christian Reconquest, and the present walls date from the reign of King Dinis (1261–1325). From the rampart walk there are superb views over Tavira's ornate chimneys, rooftops and church towers, and to the few short stretches of the town's medieval walls that survived the 1755 earthquake.

- Calçada de Paio Peres Correia
- Daily 9–5:30
- Few
- Free

IGREJA DE SANTA MARIA DO CASTELO

Standing alongside the castle, Tavira's parish church incorporates the minaret of the town's Moorish mosque, remodelled to form the clock tower. Inside are the fine 13th-century tombs of seven knights of the crusading Order of St James, whose ambush and murder prompted the Christian reconquest of the city. In addition to the fine tilework and gilded altar surrounds, the sacristy has a small museum displaying vestments and chalices.

- Calçada de Paio Peres Correia
- Apr–Oct, daily 10–12:30, 2–6; Nov–Mar daily 2–6. Closed public hols
- Few
- Free

IGREJA DE SÃO PAULO

Entered through a classical portico, more like a Greek temple than a church, St Paul's is unusual for the heavy, dark woodwork of its two side altars, ornately carved but not covered in gold. The fine collection of religious statues includes a delicate 15th-century Flemish *Virgin*.

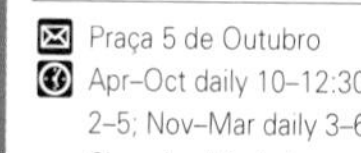

- Praça 5 de Outubro
- Apr–Oct daily 10–12:30, 2–5; Nov–Mar daily 3–6. Closed public hols
- Few
- Free

ILHA DE TAVIRA

This 10km-long island, with its sandy beaches and sheltered bathing, is the most accessible of the barrier islands in the Ria Formosa Nature Reserve (➤ 26). Ferries make the short crossing from the Quatro Águas jetty, on the south bank of the River Gilão. You can also walk to the island across the footbridge from Santa Luzia, the seafront fishing village 3km west of Tavira.

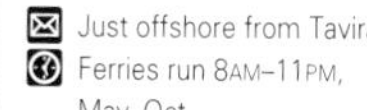

- Just offshore from Tavira
- Ferries run 8AM–11PM, May–Oct
- Cafes (£) at northeastern tip of island
- Free

What to See in Eastern Algarve

ALCOUTIM 

29F3
40km north of Vila Real de Santo António
O Soeiro café (£)
Castro Marim (➤ 82)
Praça da República
281 546179

Above: *castle walls guard the border with Spain in Alcoutim*

Alcoutim has the atmosphere of a timeless town. Life here moves at the pace of the horse-drawn ploughs that are still used to till the surrounding fields. Ferrymen frequent the O Soeiro café, just above the quay, and take passengers across the river to San Lúcar in Spain on request. There are no border controls, so it is easy to slip across the river.

Both towns are dominated by their castle. Sanlúcar's is the biggest – a massive structure crowning the cone-shaped hill above the town – but Alcoutim's is the oldest. The excavated remains of Roman structures have been overlain by 11th-century Moorish remains, in turn superseded by a 1304 fortress. Both castles are a reminder of former hostilities between Spain and Portugal.

Besides Alcoutim's castle, the other good viewpoint in town is the Ermida de Nossa Senhora da Conceiço (Hermitage of Our Lady of Conception). This whitewashed church, approached via an 18th-century stone staircase, stands at the highest point in the village and allows intimate views down into the village gardens and across the flat rooftops of the simple, cube-shaped houses.

BARRANCO DO VELHO 

29D2
30km north of Faro
Several cafés (£) on the main street, including A Tia Bia (££, ➤ 98)
Cachopo (➤ 90)

In the empty hills of the Serra da Caldeirão, Barranco do Velho is one of the few settlements of any size, located at a crossroads in an elevated spot. Visitors come to refresh themselves at the cafés lining the main street before heading on towards Lisbon or south to the coast. The village is also popular with walkers and mountain bikers, who follow the broad woodland tracks that thread through the surrounding cork oak forests.

CABANAS ✪✪

Cabanas is a fast-growing resort just to the east of Tavira. It has a broad, sandy beach facing a long sandbank, with a warm and shallow lagoon providing sheltered bathing conditions that attract families with children.

A 5km-stroll along the beach leads to the fortified village of Cacela Velha, a tiny hamlet consisting of a church and a few cottages surrounded by massive walls. The perfectly preserved fortress dates from the Peninsular War of 1808–14, when Napoleonic troops invaded Portugal.

Near by, **Happy Farm** is one of the latest attractions along the coast. It offers a mini-zoo, crazy golf and boating.

29F2
5km east of Tavira
Café (£) in Cacela Velha
Buses from Tavira
Tavira (➤ 78)

Happy Farm
Cabanas
966 321021
10–dusk
Expensive

CASTRO MARIM ✪✪✪

At Castro Marim there are two huge castles to explore, spreading across the two hills that rise above the salt flats either side of this fishing town.

The main **castle**, to the north of the town, was built in 1319 as the headquarters of the crusading Order of the Knights of Christ, founded in 1119 as the Knights Templar. The knights played a decisive role in the Christian Reconquest of Portugal. The older medieval castle is now entirely contained within the walls of its 17th-century successor, which is six times larger.

A rampart walk allows visitors to walk all the way round the castle, with views down to the fishermen's houses below, built with flat roofs for drying fish. Also within the castle walls are the offices of the Castro Marim Nature Reserve, from where walk leaflets are available.

The **São Sebastião fortress**, on the opposite hill, dates from the 17th century and is part of a much bigger complex of defensive walls that survive only in parts around the town. Like its medieval counterpart, the fortress served as a base from where to defend the entrance to the River Guadiana, bearing the brunt of hostilities between Portugal and Spain. Today, the two countries have abolished their common border and the modern suspension bridge, which crosses the river, carries the IP1 motorway, 2km northeast of the town.

29F2
4km north of Vila Real de Santo António
Cafés (£) in Rua de São Sebastião
Buses from Vila Real de Santo António
Praça 1 de Maio
281 531232

Castelo and São Sebastiao fortress
Apr–Oct 9–7; Nov–Mar 9–5. Closed public hols
Free

Castro Marim's walls, a formidable defence

The Salt Pans of Castro Marim

Salt pans backed by the bridge linking Spain and Portugal

The castle walls in Castro Marim look down on acres of salt pans, many of them in use since pre-Roman times. Now protected as a nature reserve, these salt pans, and the tidal creeks that run through them, are home to many species of bird. Take binoculars with you.

Park by a ruined building, down a track off the road, on the right, 1.4km south of Castro Marim towards Vila Real de Santo António (it's easily missed). Walking away from the main road, follow the raised path that threads through the reserve, with the main channel of the fish-filled creek to your left.

On your right, the flower-filled fields are planted with olive trees, where storks nest. These huge birds may flap lazily overhead from time to time. Also visible are egrets, dipping their beaks in the silt at the edge of the salt pans in search of food, and the occasional shy flamingo. If you tire of the heat (there are no trees and no shade on this walk) you can retrace your steps. Alternatively, you can follow the path all the way round the reserve. At its westernmost point it passes the still-working salt pans at Aroucas, where salt obtained by evaporation is piled up in a great pyramidal heap.

From here the path turns southwards, almost to the suburbs of Monte Gordo, visible (but not accessible) across the Carrasqueira estuary. The path follows the northern bank of the estuary, over several footbridges, before rejoining the outward path: turn to the right to return to the car park.

Distance
8km

Time
3 hours

Start/end point
Roadside car park, 1.4km south of Castro Marim on the western side of the road to Vila Real de Santo António
29F2

Lunch
Restaurante Pão Quente (£)
Rua de São Bartolomeu Sul, Castro Marim
281 513033

COVA DOS MOUROS PARQUE MINEIRO ✪✪✪

The open-air Mining Park at Cova dos Mouros is well signposted as you drive south along the N506 road from Martinlongo, to Vaqueiros. Located in the empty, scrub-covered hills of the northern Algarve, this museum has been created around the spoil tips and shafts of an abandoned copper mine that has been in use for more than 5,000 years. The workings were rediscovered in 1865 and have only recently been developed into this unusual attraction – now designated an ecological park.

The park centres on the reconstruction of a Chalcolithic village (2,500 BC), which re-creates the lifestyle of the very first miners. Staff, dressed in animal skins, work the ground with copies of ancient tools.

After you have learned about the mining activities, Cova dos Mouros offers other ways to spend a pleasant few

29E3
10km southeast of Martinlongo, 2km south of Vaqueiros
289 999229
Café on site
Apr–Oct 10:30–6; Nov–Mar 10:30–4:30. Closed 18 Dec to 20 Jan
Few
Expensive
Cachopo (➤ 90)

Mining heritage brought to life at Cova dos Mouros

Above: *earthquake survivor – Luz da Tavira's Manueline church*

Right: *the San Cristo chapel in Moncarapacho.* Inset: *the museum next door is home to a remarkable collection of artefacts, including Roman masonry and Napoleonic cannon balls*

hours. The park is one of several across Spain and Portugal that works for the survival of the Iberian donkey. Once so numerous as beasts of burden, these gentle, hardy creatures have now almost disappeared throughout the peninsula. Children will enjoy the rides they give across the surrounding countryside.

If you prefer to use your own energy, there are posted walks where you can take in the upland flora and fauna. In spring copious wild flowers, including rare orchids, blanket the ground, and even in the height of summer butterflies and lizards provide interest as you stroll. Finally, you can enjoy a cooling dip in the natural pools of the Foupana River and you may catch a glimpse of a family of otters.

LUZ DA TAVIRA ✪✪

- 29E2
- 7km west of Tavira
- Cafés (£) in the main street in nearby Tavira
- Tavira (➤ 78)

Not to be confused with Luz in Western Algarve (➤ 36), Luz da Tavira has one of the few churches in the Algarve to survive the 1755 earthquake. Dating from the 16th century, it is dedicated to Nossa Senhora da Luz (Our Lady of Light), whose statue fills the niche above the large, imposing, Renaissance-style porch. To the side is another porch with the stone-rope mouldings typical of the Manueline style of the early 16th century, inspired by nautical themes. The altar surround is 16th century, as are the polychromatic *azulejos* on the steps and pavement.

The houses in Luz are worth a second glance: many have the distinctive traditional *platibanda* borders. Surrounding the doors and window frames, and sometimes running along the eaves and down the house corners, these ornate plasterwork bands are decorated with floral and geometrical motifs, often picked out in a colour that contrasts with that of the exterior walls. The chimneys are unusual, too: their filigree patterns reflect the art nouveau style popular in the early 20th century, when many of these houses were built or modernised.

MONCARAPACHO ✪✪

This small, roadside town would be of little interest to visitors had not the local parish priest (who died in 1996) built up a remarkable small museum alongside the baroque Santo Cristo chapel (follow signs to **'Museu'**). It is filled with a collection of curiosities that offer a profile of the history and archaeology of the whole region: there are coins, stones from an old olive press, shackles once used to imprison African slaves, Napoleonic cannon balls, and clay scoops from Moorish-style water wheels. Among the Roman masonry, there are soldier's tombstones and a milestone that once stood alongside the main road from Faro to Seville.

Upstairs, pride of place goes to a beautiful, 18th-century Neopolitan crib scene, with lively figures of shepherds and kings, made from wood and porcelain. Alongside the museum, the tiny 16th-century chapel is covered in 17th-century *azulejos*.

The main church in the town centre has an exceptional Renaissance façade carved with the Annunciation, St Peter and St Paul, and scenes from the Passion of Christ. Animated hunchbacked figures torment Christ as helmeted soldiers prepare to scourge him. The perfectly preserved Renaissance interior has classical columns, painted with swirling red and blue acanthus-leaf patterns.

29E2
8km northeast of Olhão
Few
Cafés (£) around the main square
Buses from Olhão
Olhão (➤ 86)

Museu
Mon–Fri 11–5
Moderate

29F2
5km southwest of Vila Real de Santo António
Cafés (£) along Avenida Infante Dom Henrique
Buses from Vila Real de Santo António
Avenida Marginal 281 544495
Vila Real de Santo António (➤ 88)

Opposite: *fishing is a core element in the Algarvian economy*
Below: *Olhão's distinctive red-turreted fish market*

MONTE GORDO 

Separated from the beach by a wide, café-lined avenue, the hotels of Monte Gordo look down on one of the Algarve's finest beaches – a vast, broad sweep of golden sand. Numerous seasonal seafood restaurants and cafés, housed in makeshift timber cabins, sit along the sands, offering fresh fish provided by the local fishermen.

With its warm waters, gentle offshore breezes and endless sands, Monte Gordo is a popular place for novice windsurfers to take their first tentative lessons, and there are plenty of beachside businesses offering watersports equipment and tuition. The nightlife is very lively and cosmopolitan, with folk dance evenings, a casino, and all-night Spanish discos. Spain is a short drive away across the road bridge that crosses the River Guadiana, and local tour agents offer day trips to Seville, about two hours' drive to the east.

29E1
8km east of Faro
Cafés (£) near the market
Bus station on Avenida General Humberto Delgado 289 702157. Buses to Cacela, Faro, Fuzeta, Moncarapacho, Monte Gordo, Tavira, Vila Real de Santo António
Largo Sebastião Martins Mestre 8A 289 713936

Museu da Cidade
Edifício do Compromisso Maritimo
289 700134

OLHÃO 

Olhão is, along with Portimão, the biggest of the Algarve's fishing ports, and the eastern end of the town is dominated by warehouses and canning factories. The fish market along the seafront, with its patterned brick walls and corner turrets, has been modernised to meet EU health regulations, but has lost none of its vital character. Equally colourful is the fruit and vegetable market, its stalls piled high with dried figs, almonds, honey, herbs and local cheeses, as well as fresh fruits.

On the opposite side of the seafront promenade Olhão has some of the Algarve's most attractive and ornate buildings, with curvaceous balconies, decorated with wrought-iron flowers and acorn finials. One fine group of buildings lines the same square that houses the tourist information centre, one block from the seafront, and there are more in the streets radiating north – look above the shop façades in the main commercial streets to take in the detail. A maze of cobbled pedestrian-only streets leads to the town's main church, Igreja Matriz, with its marvellously theatrical baroque façade. Inside, life-size angels flank the splendid, gilded altar. Behind the church, the newly opened **Museu da Cidade** holds temporary exhibitions and there is a small gallery displaying prehistoric and Roman finds.

RESERVA NATURAL DA RIA FORMOSA (➤ 26, TOP TEN)

SÃO BRÁS DE ALPORTEL ✪✪

São Brás is a prosperous market town sandwiched between the scenic Serra da Monte Figo region and the Serra do Caldeirão to the north. The area is renowned for its almond orchards, which blossom from late December to early March. A good spot from where to view the fertile countryside is the tombstone-flagged terrace of the largely rebuilt 15th-century church, Igreja Matriz, which contains some lively 18th-century paintings and statues of the Archangel Gabriel and St Euphemia. Two blocks east of the church, the building that once served as the summer palace of the Bishops of Faro is fronted by an attractive domed pavilion, which shelters the eight-spouted Episcopal Fountain.

The **Museu Etnográfico do Traje Algarvio** (Algarvian Ethnographic Costume Museum) lies one block north in the former home of a wealthy 19th-century cork merchant. The displays of clothing, furniture and domestic objects illustrate various aspects of Algarvian rural life, and the farm buildings alongside house a collection of agricultural implements and old vehicles.

29E2
13km east of Loulé
Mon–Fri
Cafés (£) around Largo do Igreja and Largo do Mercado
Buses from Faro
Rua Dr Evaristo Sousa Gago 1 289 842211
Faro (► 62)

Museu Etnográfico do Traje Algarvio

Rua Dr José Dias Sancho 59
289 842618
Mon–Fri 10–1, 2–5; Sat and Sun 2–5. Closed public hols
Few
Moderate

VILA REAL DE SANTO ANTÓNIO

29F2
At the eastern edge of the Algarve, 23km east of Tavira
Cafés (£) in Praça Marquês de Pombal and pedestrian streets north of the square
Bus station on Avenida Casal Ribeiro (281 511807) with services to and from Altura, Cacela, Castro Marim, Faro, Manta Rota, Monte Gordo, Olhão and Tavira
Castro Marim (► 82)

Ayamonte
29F2
In Spain, on opposite bank of River Guadiana to Vila Real
Cafés (£) and restaurants (£) in Plaza de la Ligna

Centro Cultural António Aleixo
Rua Dr Teófilo Braga 38
Mon–Fri 10–1, 3–7
Free

Vila Real was founded by Royal Charter in 1773 and represents the town planning ideals of the Marquês de Pombal (1699–1782), Portugal's chief minister under King José I (1714–77). It was the Marquês, virtually exercising absolute power, who expelled the Jesuits from Portugal and swept away many church-based institutions. He planned this city to represent the rational ideals of the Enlightenment, in contrast to the Spanish city of Ayamonte on the opposite bank of the River Guadiana.

Ayamonte has prospered, as shown by its gleaming white tower blocks and modern port facilities, while charming Vila Real remains in a time warp. Vila Real's riverside embankment is lined by grand hotels and scores of restaurants and shops catering for the Spanish bargain hunters who come here to buy household goods, tempted by low prices.

One block inland from the river embankment, the legacy of the Marquês de Pombal is evident in the strict grid of streets and the geometrical precision of the elegant main square, Praça Marquês de Pombal, with its church, town hall and former infantry barracks. In the centre of the square, the obelisk monument to King José I acts like the needle of a giant sundial, casting its shadow on the traditional black and white mosaic paving.

In 1991, a new suspension bridge opened across the River Guadiana, linking Portugal to Spain, but the river ferry continues to do a brisk trade, plying the river at roughly half-hourly intervals, from 9 until 9. You do not need a passport to visit **Ayamonte** (Spain and Portugal have abolished their common borders) and this is a good way of sampling the different cultures of the two countries (don't forget that Spain is usually an hour ahead of Portugal, and that almost everything shuts for the siesta during the afternoon, from 1 to 4).

Across the river from Vila Real, Ayamonte's white towers gleam

By contrast with the monochrome Pombeline style of Vila Real, Ayamonte seems the more colourful town of the two, with its flower-filled streets and its lavishly tiled façades. It is also a town with many art galleries and studios displaying the work of contemporary artists, attracted by the lucid air and bold colours of the Costa del Luz (Coast of Light).

Did you know ?

Vila Real de Santo António was built in just five months, using the same techniques developed by the Marquês de Pombal in rebuilding Lisbon after the 1755 earthquake – building materials were brought to the site by boat, including timbers and masonry already cut and dressed, ready to use.

Ayamonte does not have the monopoly on modern art, however. Back in Vila Real, the **Centro Cultural António Aleixo** contains a gallery of works by Manuel Cabanas, a renowned local painter and engraver whose woodcuts of Algarvian life in the 1950s are fascinating.

The Praça Marquês de Pombal, with its obelisk, resembles a giant sundial

Eastern Highlights

Distance
160km

Time
1 day

Start/end point
Tavira
29E2

Lunch
O Soeiro (£)
Rua do Município 4, Alcoutim
281 546241

Cork oak, grown for its bark, flourishes in the hills of inland Algarve

Explore the empty hills of the Serra do Caldeirão, with their abandoned windmills and scattered cork oaks, then follow the scenic Guadiana River.

From Tavira, head north on the N397 for 33km to Cachopo.

The countryside consists largely of shallow, acidic schistic soils that are not very fertile, though cork oaks thrive. In between the forests are hills covered in wild cistus and holly oak. Cachopo produces sheep's milk cheese and sweet, air-cured mountain hams.

Continue north on the N124 for 16km to Martinlongo, then south on the N506 for 12km to Vaqueiros.

Just north of Vaqueiros, visit the Cova dos Mouros mine, which was worked from the Copper Age (3500 BC) onwards and is now an industrial museum (➤ 83).

Continue a short way south, then turn left (east), signposted Melhedes/Soudes and continue for 18km to the junction with the N122; head left (north) for 13km to the junction with the N124, then right (east) on the N124 for 6km to Alcoutim.

Stop for lunch in Alcoutim (➤ 80), then explore the castle.

Head south on the road that follows the River Guadiana.

Look out for the Roman ruins lying by the roadside just as you enter Montinho das Laranjeiras, immediately before the bridge; the remains consist of a villa and an early Christian church, with apse and stone-lined graves. In Guerreiros do Rio, stop to visit the former school, which now houses a small river museum.

When the river road meets the N122, turn left (south) and continue for 8km to Azinhal, noted for its lacework. Approaching Castro Marim (➤ 81), there are views to the left of the suspension bridge carrying the IP1 motorway across the River Guadiana to Seville, in southern Andalucia. To return quickly to Tavira, join the motorway here and head west.

Where To...

Above: fado *singers*
Right: *typical* cataplana *dish*

Western Algarve

Prices
Prices are approximate, based on a three-course meal for one without drinks and service:

£ = under €13
££ = €13–€20
£££ = over €20

Opening Hours
Most restaurants in the Algarve open from 10AM through to midnight, though smarter restaurants may close between 3 and 7, and some open only in the evening.

Barão de São João

Cangalho (££)
Rustic Portuguese cuisine is the speciality of this rural restaurant, located in a traditional farmhouse. The home-baked bread comes fresh from a wood-fired clay oven, as does the roast suckling pig, chicken *cabidela* and hunter's rabbit.
Quinta Figueiras, Sítio do Medronho 282 687218 Lunch, dinner. Closed Mon

Burgau

Ancora (££)
Enjoy sea views with your food, choosing from an adventurous menu: mussels cooked in Indian spices and pork in a fig sauce are among the imaginative offerings.
Largo dos Pescadores 282 697102 Dinner. Closed Mon in summer, Mon and Tue in winter

Beach Bar (£)
Rock-bottom prices at this well-positioned beachside restaurant, with its seafront terrace, specialising in grilled fresh fish.
Praia de Burgau 282 697553 Lunch, dinner. Closed Mon

Cabeça do Porco (££)
The porcine theme at the Pig's Head is reflected in the décor of this English-style pub, and in the very popular pig roasts, served on Sundays. Portuguese, English and international dishes are on the menu during the rest of the week.
Luz road, east of Burgau 282 697315 Lunch, dinner

Caravela (£££)
Upmarket Portuguese cuisine, in the attractive surroundings of a palm-shaded garden. Rabbit hunter-style and roast saddle of lamb cooked in mountain herbs are popular.
Rua Direita 282 69274 Dinner

Casa Grande (££)
Set in the former winery attached to a beautifully restored manor house, this restaurant serves Portuguese and vegetarian dishes. Reservations advised.
On the Burgau to Praia da Luz road 282 697416 Dinner. Closed Dec–Feb

Carrapateira

Sítio do Forno (££)
Wonderful panoramic views of Amado beach from the terrace of this cliff-side restaurant, which specialises in barbecue fish caught in the family boat.
Praia do Amado 963 558404 Lunch, dinner. Closed Mon

O Sítio do Rio (££)
On the edge of Bordeira beach, this popular restaurant has a more varied menu than Sítio do Forno but the view isn't as spectacular.
Praia Bordeira (on the coastal road) 282 973119 Lunch, dinner. Closed Mon

Lagos

Dom Sebastião (££)
This popular restaurant, with its timbered ceiling, also has an open-air terrace and an extensive menu.
Rua 25 de Abril 282 762795 Lunch, dinner. Closed Sun in winter

Mediterraneo (££)
Vegetarians will find plenty of choice at this friendly restaurant with a shady terrace.
Rua da Senhora da Graça 282 768476 Lunch, dinner

No Pátio (££)
Scandinavian and Portuguese dishes vie for attention on the menu of this beautiful old town-house restaurant, with its peaceful patio garden.
Rua Lançarote de Freitas 46 282 763777 Dinner. Closed Mon all year and Sun Nov–May

O Arcos (££)
O Arcos serves the best in seafood, including live lobsters and traditional Portuguese dishes. It has tables on the square and a large indoor dining room.
Rua 25 Abril, 30 282 763210 Lunch, dinner. Closed Mon

Praia da Luz

Fortaleza da Luz (££)
The remains of the town's 16th-century fortress have been turned into a popular and characterful restaurant with coastal views. Fresh fish, Portuguese cuisine and flambé dishes, plus live jazz on Sundays.
Rua da Igreja 3 282 789926 Lunch, dinner. Closed mid-Nov to mid-Dec

O Poço (££)
This restaurant overlooking the beach has an international menu, as well as local specialities.
Avenida dos Pescadores (on the seafront) 282 789189 Lunch, dinner

Sagres

A Tasca (££)
Located on the harbour in Sagres, in a building that once served as a market, and specialising in fresh fish, including lobster and clams *amêijoas*.
Sagres harbour 282 624177 Lunch, dinner

Bossa Nova (£)
Pasta and pizzas, plus vegetarian dishes and seafood at this friendly and moderately priced restaurant.
Rua da Mareta 282 624566 Lunch, dinner

Fortaleza do Beliche (££)
An upmarket Portuguese restaurant in the atmospheric setting of a fortress destroyed by Sir Francis Drake in 1587 and restored in the 1960s.
5km southeast of Sagres on the road to Cabo de São Vicente 282 624734 Lunch, dinner

Pousada do Infante (££)
Luxuriate in the comfortable ambience of this hotel restaurant serving locally caught fish, set on a cliff-top with sweeping views.
Atalaia Point 282 624222 Lunch, dinner

Vila do Bispo

Café Correia (£)
A simple, rustic, typically Portuguese restaurant that specialises in serving barnacles. Fish is predominent on the extended menu and wine is served from the cask.
Rua 1 de Maio 4 282 760985 Lunch, dinner. Closed Sat

Bars and *Pastelarias*
Bars are usually open all day, from early in the morning until late at night, serving coffee, soft drinks and alcohol. Most serve cheese, ham or *presunto* (cured ham) sandwiches, and there will usually be a small display of cakes. Just about every village, no matter how small, has a bar, so you are never very far from refreshment. The *pastelaria* is one step up: usually attached to a bakery, it serves a much more extensive range of cakes, as well as savoury snacks, such as quiche or salads, hot dogs and hamburgers. More often found in towns and cities than in villages, the *pastelaria* is where many city-dwelling Portuguese eat lunch, and most close at 7, as the smarter restaurants begin to open.

Appetisers
When you eat in an Algarvian restaurant, the waiter will present you with a basket of delicious homemade bread, along with a selection of spreads – butter, cheese and sardine paste are the commonest – which many Portuguese will have instead of a starter. Some restaurants also serve home-cured olives and a range of nibbles – such as chopped vegetables dressed with garlic, herbs and oil – which make a delicious accompaniment to pre-dinner drinks.

Western Central Algarve

Fish on the Menu
Your favourite fish may not seem so familiar if the menu only has their names in Portuguese. Here is a short list of fish that you will frequently find on Algarvian menus: *atum* (tuna), *bacalhau* (salted cod), *cherne* (sea bass), *carapau* (mackerel), *pargo* (bream), *salmão* (salmon), *salmonete* (red mullet), *truta* (trout) and *espadarte* (swordfish).

Algoz

O João (££)

In this restaurant you will be surrounded by local people who come to enjoy hearty Portuguese specialities. It's especially atmospheric at lunchtime, when the workers come in from surrounding towns.

Senhora do Pilar (on the same street as the Hermitage) 282 575332 Lunch, dinner

Alvor

Somewhere Else (££)

Fun restaurant with Irish and Dutch owners where you cook your own meat or fresh fish on heated lava stones.

Rua Poeta João de Deus 282 458595 Lunch, dinner

Armação de Pêra

Santola Restaurant (£££)

Pretty restaurant next to the castle chapel, with a terrace overlooking the beach – great for a relaxed dinner. Fresh seafood is the speciality, with live lobster and crab on offer.

Largo de Fortaleza 082 312332 Lunch, dinner

Caldas de Monchique

Termas de Monchique (£££)

An upmarket restaurant within the refurbished spa complex, with a beautiful formal dining room and large sun-drenched terrace where you can enjoy a long lunch, romantic dinner or quick snack. It has an international menu, with fine wine and cigars.

Caldas de Monchique 282 910910 Lunch, dinner

Carvoeiro

Grande Muralha (££)

This Sino-Portuguese restaurant has familiar and not-so-familiar dishes on its menu. The not-so-familiar include curried squid and fried ice cream. For something more down-to-earth, try the delicious sizzling prawns.

Estrada do Farol, Praia do Carvoeiro 282 357380 Lunch, dinner

Le Bistroquet (££)

Small bistro-style French restaurant in the centre of Carvoeiro, with friendly service from the Dutch management.

Estrada do Farol, Praia do Carvoeiro 282 357743 Lunch, dinner. Closed Mon

Ferragudo

Sueste (££)

Fresh fish is a speciality of this restaurant, at the end of the fishing docks. Sit outside and look over the river estuary or eat in the dining room, with its 17th-century painted ceiling.

Rua da Ribeira 91 282 461945 Lunch, dinner. Closed Mon

Lagoa

Casa Velha (££)

Come here on a Saturday night for live *fado* music, but be sure to book in advance. Set in a converted bakery, adorned by the paintings of the owner's artist wife, this popular restaurant serves African-influenced dishes, such as Angolan prawns and chicken moamba, alongside Algarvian staples.

Rua Mouzinho de Albuquerque 60 282 342600 Lunch, dinner

Monchique

Bica-Boa (££)

This is one of the Algarve's best restaurants, serving good regional and international food.

Estrada de Lisboa 282 912271 Lunch, dinner

Paraíso da Montanha (£)

Visitors flock to this restaurant for its excellent chicken *piri-piri*, and the mountain views.

Estrada da Fóia 282 912150 Lunch, dinner

Quinta de São Bento (£££)

The views from this award-winning restaurant vie for attention with the grandeur of the building – the former summer residence of the royal House of Bragança – located near the summit of Fóia, the Algarve's highest peak. The menu specialises in game and also offers wild boar.

Estrada da Fóia 282 912143 Lunch, dinner

Portimão

Dona Barca (£)

One of the best of Portimão's renowned fish restaurants, in a converted riverside warehouse. It serves fish straight off the boats and has live music in summer.

Largo da Barca 282 484189 Lunch, dinner

A Máscara (££)

A rare find anywhere, this restaurant serves excellent Indonesian food, vegetarian dishes and Balinese satay. Some Thai dishes as well. Live music.

Rua de Santa Isabel 282 422072 Dinner. Closed Sun

Praia da Rocha

Casa de Rocha (££)

With three terraces giving stunning views of the coastline, the Casa de Rocha makes a great place for a sunset meal. Traditional Portuguese dishes are served in this former summerhouse.

Avenida Tomás Cabreira 282 419674 Lunch, dinner

Shang Hai (££)

This and its sister restaurant (Bamboo Garden, Loja 1, Edificio Lamego, Avenida Tomás Cabreira) make the most of the fresh local seafood. Deep-fried ice cream is the signature dish.

Loja 2, Edifício Cruzeiro 282 416601 Lunch, dinner

Silves

Café Inglês (£)

Opposite the cathedral and alongside the castle entrance, this café is in an elegant 1920s house originally built as the residence of the mayor. Enjoy home-baked bread and cakes with afternoon tea or more substantial Portuguese and English snacks.

Escadas do Castello 11 282 442585 Lunch, dinner. Closed Sat

Casa Velha de Silves (££)

Overshadowed by the gates to the old Moorish city, the Casa Velha offers traditional Portuguese grilled fish, *cataplana* (fish stew) and *espetada* (kebabs). The restaurant holds regular concerts of *fado* and other folk music.

Rua 25 de Abril 13 282 445491 Lunch, dinner

Accompaniments

You do not normally need to order vegetables or salad separately with your main course. The dish will automatically be served with a selection of cooked seasonal vegetables, or a small salad of grated carrots and cabbage, with tomato and cucumber. Chips are the traditional accompaniment to meat dishes, and boiled potatoes are served with fish, unless you request otherwise.

Eastern Central Algarve

Algarvian Wine
Local wines are inexpensive and quite strong – especially the reds, which are typically 13 or 13.5% alcohol. They are sold mostly as *vinho da casa* and, in traditional Portuguese restaurants, are drawn from a barrel. If you want a bottle of local wine, look for the Lagoa label. Wine experts tend to dismiss Algarvian wines, saying they lack subtlety. Softer and fuller flavoured wines come from the Alentejo, and are sold under the names of the co-operative producers, Borba, Redondo and Reguengos de Monsaraz.

Albufeira

La Travessa (££)
Friendly service and good value is the signature of this cosy restaurant down a covered lane just east of the Rua 5 de Outubro.
Travessa dos Arcos 78 289 513299 Lunch, dinner

O Penedo (££)
Delicious garlic clams are the speciality of this popular cliff-top restaurant.
Rua Latino Coelho 15 289 587429 Lunch, dinner

Almancil

Casa de Portuguesa (££)
One of the prettiest restaurants on the Algarve, with an interior of stucco and *azulejos*, the Casa de Portuguesa is family-friendly and serves excellent local cuisine.
Vale Formosa (on the road to Areeiro) 289 393301 Lunch, dinner. Closed Mon

São Gabriel (£££)
One of a cluster of fine restaurants in the Almancil area, São Gabriel has earned a Michelin star. Reservations necessary.
Lobo/Quinta do Lago 289 394521 Dinner. Closed Mon

La Paella (££)
If you have tried *arroz do marisco* (Portuguese seafood rice), come here to find out how it compares with the Spanish favourite *paella*. For those with smaller appetites, the restaurant serves a range of *tapas*.
Estrada de Vale d'Aguas 26 289 393874 Lunch, dinner

Alte

Fonte Pequeña Restaurant/Bar (£)
Large restaurant with wood-panelled dining room and terraces overlooking the stream and springs. There is a wood fire in winter. The menu includes hearty meat dishes and a range of snacks.
Fonte Pequiña 289 478509 Lunch

Faro

Aliança (£)
The food is unexciting and the service slow at this traditional Portuguese café, one of the oldest in the country, but people come for the ambience of the dimly lit, wood-panelled 1920s interior, and to sit where statesmen and philosophers, including Simone de Beauvoir, have sat.
Praça Francisco Gomes 6 289 801621 Lunch

Cidade Velha (££)
Atmospheric town-house restaurant in the old city close to the cathedral and archaeological museum. Imaginative menu includes fresh clams steamed with coriander, dates wrapped in bacon, and prawns in beer.
Rua Domingos Guieiro 19 289 827145 Lunch, dinner

Mesa dos Mouros (£££)
A pretty converted house in the cathedral square is home to this bijou restaurant with a small terrace. Inside, the small rooms are soothed by classical music.
Largo da Sé 10 289 878873 Lunch, dinner. Closed Sun

Sol y Jardim (£)

Excellent traditional cuisine, particularly the *cataplanas* (fish stew). Come here for a taste and feel of old Portugal.

✉ Praça Ferreira de Almeida 22–23 ☎ 289 823337 ⌚ Lunch, dinner. Closed Sun

Loulé

Bica Velha (£££)

Located in a characterful medieval building, claimed to be the oldest in Loulé, this excellent restaurant has a varied menu of local fish, served with style. Book ahead.

✉ Rua Martim Moniz 17–19 ☎ 289 463376 ⌚ Dinner

O Avenida Velha (££)

This distinguished old restaurant is famous for its homemade bread, and small savoury dishes, similar to Spanish *tapas*.

✉ Avenida José da Costa Mealha 40, first floor ☎ 289 462106 ⌚ Lunch, dinner. Closed Sun

Museu do Lagar (££)

A traditional Portuguese restaurant in the cathedral square, with dishes including wild boar, ostrich and buffalo. The huge vaulted interior makes for great atmosphere.

✉ Largo da Matriz 7 ☎ 289 416307 ⌚ Lunch, dinner. Closed Sun

Quarteira

Adega do Peixe (£)

Spacious, good-value restaurant specialising in charcoal-grilled seafood and typical Portuguese dishes.

✉ Avenida Infante de Sagres ☎ 289 388370 ⌚ Lunch, dinner

Sea Horse (£)

Good-value family restaurant, with pancakes and traditional fish dishes on the menu.

✉ Avenida Infante de Sagres ☎ 289 313074 ⌚ Lunch, dinner

Querença

Restaurante de Querença (££)

While away the long siesta hours in this restaurant, in the main square of a tiny hilltop village, or enjoy a dinner with accordion music at weekends. Rabbit and wild boar appear on the menu, as well as fish kebabs and lamb dishes. Book at weekends.

✉ Largo da Igreja ☎ 289 422540 ⌚ Lunch, dinner. Closed Wed

Quinta do Lago

Casa do Golfe (£££)

Modern bistro-style restaurant with a large terrace overlooking a driving range. Short menu of grilled meat and fish.

✉ Avenida André Jordan ☎ 289 356087 ⌚ Lunch, dinner

Vale do Lobo

Memories of China (£££)

The Algarve branch of the late Ken Lo's famous chain of upmarket Chinese restaurants. Faultless food, including the delicious sizzling three-seafood platter.

✉ David Lloyd Tennis Centre, Vale do Lobo ☎ 289 393939 ⌚ Dinner. Closed Sat

Vilamoura

Golden Ming (££)

Popular Chinese restaurant alongside the marina. Book a table in summer.

✉ Marina Plaza ☎ 289 301082 ⌚ Lunch, dinner

Desserts

Two desserts that you will invariably find on the menu are *tarte* and *pudim*. *Tarte* can be made with many different ingredients, but nearly all have ground almonds as their base, mixed with flour and egg, poured into a pastry case and baked until golden. Some are additionally flavoured with lemon juice or honey syrup. *Pudim* is crème caramel, but not the individual servings you might expect in a French restaurant: Portuguese *pudim* is a substantial ring of steamed egg custard from which slices are cut to order. A more unusual choice, if you can find it, is *queijo de figo* – literally 'fig cheese' – made from layers of dried figs, ground almonds, cinnamon and chocolate.

Eastern Algarve

Regional Variations
In coastal regions, grilled fresh fish predominates, and regular deliveries to even the most distant inland village means that it is also a major element on their menus, though not in such great variety. Inland you are more likely to find lamb, kid, pork and chicken, while restaurants in the Barrocal mountains will often have a section of the menu devoted to game: wild boar, quail, partridge, hare and rabbit in particular. Perhaps the most distinctive cuisine is that of the Guadiana River valley, where the river itself is the source of the eels, lampreys and mullet that are typical of local restaurants.

Alcoutim

O Soeiro (£)
Tucked into a shady corner beside the parish church, O Soeiro is often frequented by local ferrymen waiting for passengers wanting to cross to Spain. From tables on the terrace there are river views, and you can watch your chicken or pork being grilled over a charcoal brazier.
✉ Rua do Município 4 ☎ 281 546241 🕐 Lunch. Closed Sat and Sun

Ti Afonso (£)
Very good and busy restaurant serving Portuguese meat dishes. Not as pretty as O Soeiro – no river view – but the food and atmosphere make up for that.
✉ Praça da República ☎ 967 292169 🕐 Lunch, dinner. Closed Mon

Barranco do Velho

A Tia Bia (££)
This fine restaurant is often packed with hungry walkers and cyclists who come to enjoy the rare landscape of the forested Serra do Caldeirão mountains. Specialising in game dishes, the restaurant often has wild boar on the menu, as well as partridge with cabbage, and pumpkin with rabbit.
✉ Barranco do Velho crossroads ☎ 289 846425 🕐 Lunch, dinner

Monte Gordo

O Cruzeiro
A choice location and appetising menu combine to make this an excellent venue for a leisurely meal.
✉ Praia de Monte Gordo ☎ 281 542288 🕐 Lunch, dinner. Closed Wed

Dourado (££)
One of a group of timber shacks on the beach at Monte Gordo, with shaded terraces serving *cataplana* (fish stew) and a wide range of other traditional Portuguese dishes.
✉ Avenida Infante Dom Henrique ☎ 281 512202 🕐 Lunch, dinner

Goa (££)
Reliable standard curry house serving southern Indian food, majoring in delicate fish curries with coconut and fruits.
✉ Rua Fernando Pó ☎ 281 512606 🕐 Dinner

Olhão

O Bote (££)
Across the street from the market, this restaurant serves delicious grilled meat and fish. It has a small terrace but large indoor dining area.
✉ Avenida 5 de Outubro ☎ 289 721183 🕐 Lunch, dinner. Closed Sun

Santa Bárbara de Nexe

La Réserve (£££)
Much-lauded restaurant, regarded by some as the Algarve's best. Mainly French food served stylishly, but at a high price. Reservations are essential in summer.
✉ Estrada de Esteval ☎ 289 999234 🕐 Lunch, dinner. Closed Tue

São Brás de Alportel

Luís dos Frangos (£)
Locals flock here for the mouth-watering barbecued chicken, served with chips, salad and local wine.
✉ Tavira road ☎ 289 842635 🕐 Lunch, dinner

Pousada de São Brás (££)
Elegant restaurant in state-run hotel with beautiful views over wooded hills. Try *caldeirada de borrego* (lamb stew).
São Brás de Alportel 289 843205 Lunch, dinner

Tavira

Beira Rio (££)
By the old bridge, this elegant riverside restaurant has a range of vegetarian dishes and is noted for its garlic-flavoured quail. Book ahead in summer.
Rua Borda d'Água da Assêca 46–52 281 323165 Lunch, dinner. Closed last three weeks in Nov and Jan–Easter

Bica (£)
Plain, simple restaurant with a friendly atmosphere and huge portions. Try *corvina à casa* (bream in onion sauce).
Rua Almirante Cândido dos Reis 22–24 (in the Residencial Lagôas) 281 323843; reservations 281 322252 Lunch, dinner

Casa Cota (£)
Dine on the roof terrace for views over the characterful roof tops of Tavira. Specialises in charcoal-grilled meats.
Rua João Vaz Corte Real 38 281 324873 Lunch, dinner

Imperial (£££)
Grand restaurant renowned for its chicken and rice dishes, and its *serrabucho de marisco* (mixed seafood with pork).
Rua José Pires Padinha 22 281 322306 Lunch, dinner

O Pátio (££)
Push the boat out and try lobster or tiger prawns flambé, or sample something more modestly priced, such as clams *cataplana*, couscous or fish kebab, washed down with the local Taviran wine.
Rua António Cabreira 30 281 323008 Lunch, dinner

Quatro Águas (££)
It is a short step from the boat to the table for the fish and shellfish served at this atmospheric restaurant, located alongside the fish warehouse, at the junction of the rivers Gilão and Formosa.
Quatro Águas 281 325329 Lunch, dinner

Vila Real de Santo António

Caves do Guadiana (££)
Located on the banks of the Guadiana River, this restaurant specialises in Portuguese-style seafood and spicy African-style cod.
Avenida da República 89 281 544498 Lunch, dinner. Closed Thu dinner

O Coracão de Cidade (££)
Large and popular, with tables spilling on to the pavement of the pedestrianised shopping street west of the main square. The vast menu caters to the tastes of many nationalities, from English sandwiches to Spanish *tapas* by way of Andalucian *gazpacho* and squid *Sevilhana*, plus pizzas and chicken *piri-piri*.
Rua Cândido dos Reis 081 512972 Lunch, dinner

Liqueurs
Algarvians have a gift for turning their local fruits into alcoholic liqueurs. The most popular drink with which to end the meal is *medronho*, a potent spirit distilled from the strawberry-coloured fruits of the arbutus tree, which grows in profusion in the Monchique region. Lovers of almonds will adore the delicious sweet liqueur called *amêndoa amarga*, also sold as *Algarviana*. Another good choice is *brandymel*, a warming blend of brandy and honey.

Western Algarve

Prices
Prices are for a double room, including breakfast and tax:
£ = under €80
££ = €80–€120
£££ = over €120

Hotels
Many seafront hotels in the Algarve are of a very high standard, with luxurious accommodation in well-maintained gardens, overlooking a glorious beach. They are also quite expensive, though often cheaper if booked as part of a package holiday. Conversely, tour companies often charge more for the cheaper hotels than if you booked direct. Prices drop dramatically in winter and many four- and five-star hotels offer very good value, often matching the rates of much lower-class hotels. Nearly all hotels in the Algarve include breakfast as part of the room price. Half- and full-board terms are also available at the more expensive hotels.

Burgau

Casa Grande (£)
This characterful guest house is packed with antiques and collectables. Artists and writers love its faded grandeur and so will anyone searching for something different from the run-of-the-mill modern hotel.
✉ 8650 Burgau ☎ 282 697416; www.nexus-pt.com/casagrande 🕐 All year

Lagos

Golfinho (££)
Superb views of the Dona Ana beach, with its wind-sculpted rocks, from this modern 4-star hotel, with pool, restaurant and bar.
✉ Praia Dona Ana ☎ 282 769900; www.hotelgolfinho.com 🕐 All year

Praia da Luz

Belavista (££)
The Belavista sits above the sheltered beach at Praia da Luz, with its rooms grouped amphitheatre-style around the central swimming pool. The rooms are spacious and comfortable and there is plenty to do here, from scuba diving and discos for the teenagers to yoga and meditation classes.
✉ Beach road ☎ 282 788655; www.belavistadaluz.com 🕐 All year

Luz Bay Club (££)
The Luz Bay Club makes an excellent choice for those who prefer self-catering accommodation. It has two-, three- and four-bedroomed villas, along with a restaurant and other amenities. There is an adults-only pool and a fun pool with slide, tennis and squash courts. Watersports, including dinghy sailing, windsurfing and scuba diving, are also available.
✉ Avenida Pescadores, Praia da Luz, 8600 Lagos ☎ 282 788553 🕐 All year

Sagres

Fortaleza do Beliche (££)
You have to book well in advance to stay at this *pousada* (state-run hotel), but advance planning is worth it to enjoy the charm of this 16th-century fortress, sacked by Sir Francis Drake in 1587 and restored in the 1960s. Set on a cliff-top, there are wonderful views to enjoy with your meals on the terrace.
✉ 8650 Sagres ☎ 282 624124; www.pousadasofportugal.com 🕐 All year

Pousada do Infante (££)
Located on the cliff-tops, this splendid *pousada* (state-run hotel) is built in traditional Algarvian style, with red-tiled roofs, ornate chimneys and a cloister-like loggia providing shaded terraces to its rooms. Facilities include a swimming pool and tennis courts, and there is fishing and watersports in Sagres.
✉ 8650 Sagres ☎ 282 624222; www.pousadas.pt 🕐 All year

Salema

Estalagem Infante do Mar (£££)
A new resort in spacious grounds between Budens and the coastal resort of Salema. There is a range of sports and leisure facilities and it is a good location for exploring Western Algarve.
✉ Praia da Salema, 8650–193, Budens ☎ 282 690100; 🕐 All year

Western Central Algarve

Alvor

Pestana Delfim Hotel (£££)
In lush grounds above the Três Irmãos beach, the Pestana Delfim is a tower hotel, with golf and sports facilities near by. Alvor is 10 minutes' walk away.
Praia Três Irmãos, 8501-904 282 400800; www.pestana.com All year

Armação de Pêra

Vila Vita Parc (£££)
Architecturally, this is one of the more distinguished hotels in the Algarve, with its Moorish-inspired domes and shady cloisters. Facilities include six pools, a children's playground, tennis and squash courts, a 9-hole pitch-and-putt golf course, health club, beauty salon, five restaurants and a nightclub.
Apartado 196, P-8365 Armação de Pêra 282 315310; www.vilavita.com All year

Carvoeiro

Almansor (££)
Well located for a number of golf courses, the Almansor is on the cliff-tops above its own cove, which is sheltered by sandstone cliffs and reached by a path from the hotel grounds. Facilities include a pool, shops and a babysitting service.
Praia Vale Covo, Carvoeiro, 8400 Lagoa 282 358026; www.nexus-pt.com/almansor All year

Ferragudo

Casabela Hotel (£££)
Luxurious hotel in a picturesque setting above the Praia Grande beach that makes an excellent base for walking and watersports. Facilities include heated outdoor pool, tennis courts and restaurant.
Vale da Areia, Ferragudo, near Portimão 282 461580 All year

Portimão

Le Meridien Penina (£££)
The perfect family resort hotel, the Penina offers supervised activities for children in July and August, including excursions, competitions, tennis, golf, mountain biking and horse riding. Parents can take their pick of watersports, golf, tennis and horse riding.
Apartado 146, Montes de Alvor, 8502 Portimão 282 415415; www.lemeridien-hotels.com All year

Praia da Rocha

Algarve Casino (£££)
This is one of the Algarve's best hotels, with a huge range of facilities on offer, though at a price. The hotel sits on the cliff-top above Praia da Rocha beach, and many of the rooms have balconies overlooking the ocean. The Praia da Rocha casino is part of the complex, with a restaurant and nightly dinner dances and floor shows.
Praia da Rocha, 8500 Portimão 282 415001; www.solverde.pt All year

Silves

Hotel Colina dos Mouros (£)
Modern, good-value hotel in Moorish style, across the river from Silves, with wonderful views across the town. Facilities include gardens, a pool, children's pool, bar and restaurant.
8301 Silves 282 440420 All year

Self-catering

Most accommodation in the Algarve is in self-catering villas and apartments, often set in a complex around pleasant gardens, with central facilities such as a bar, swimming pool, shop and restaurant. Villas usually have a small kitchen with fridge and gas cooker, a garage and small garden, a living room with TV and simply furnished bedrooms with en suite bathrooms. A maid will clean the villa and change the linen once a week. Advance booking is essential for the main holiday period. (Travel agents' brochures are full of offers, but you can often get a higher standard of accommodation, and better prices, by renting privately.)

Eastern Central & Eastern Algarve

High and Low Season Prices

Hotel prices reflect the demand at different times of year. January and February are the cheapest, and many retired people take advantage of the very low rents on self-catering villas to escape the cold weather of northern Europe. Christmas, Easter and school half-term weeks are popular, but not greatly expensive – at this time of year the availability of flights to the Algarve is more a limiting factor than rental prices, so make arrangements well in advance. Spring comes relatively early, from late February and through March, and is one of the best times of year to visit for weather, temperature and wildlife. July and August are the hottest and by far the most expensive months.

Eastern Central Algarve

Albufeira

Albufeira Jardim Hotel (££)

Situated on high ground above the old town, the Albufeira Jardim is an aparthotel (each room has a mini-kitchen). Facilities include tennis, a pool, restaurant and café. Courtesy bus into town and the beach.

✉ Cerro de Piedade, 8200 ☎ 289 586972; www.albufeira-jardim.com 🕐 All year

Quinta da Balaia (£££)

One of the newest resort hotels along the Algarve coast and set in lush grounds, the Quinta da Balaia offers luxurious accommodation in one- to five-bedroom villas. Close to the golf course, with sporting facilities on site.

✉ Branqueira, Praia Santa Eulália, 8200-594 ☎ 289 586575 🕐 All year

Sheraton Algarve (£££)

Recently awarded Portugal's coveted Silver Medal for excellence in tourism services, the Sheraton Algarve, also known as Pinecliffs, is not just a hotel – it is a complete resort, with its own 9-hole golf course and golf academy, as well as a large outdoor pool and tennis-courts. Guests have access to miles of unbroken sand, with the beaches of Praia da Falésia right on the doorstep. Windsurfing, pedalos, jet skis and waterski facilities are all available, and there is a good choice of both casual and more formal restaurants.

✉ Praia da Falésia, 8200 Albufeira ☎ 289 500100; www.pinecliffs.com 🕐 All year

Almancil

Quinta do Lago (£££)

Quinta do Lago is in a magnificent setting on the Ria Formosa estuary. Each room has its own garden terrace and there are tennis courts, outdoor and indoor pools, a gym, sauna, solarium and masseuse. Two golf courses are alongside. The hotel hires bicycles and arranges fishing trips, waterskiing, sailing, windsurfing and canoeing.

✉ 8135 Almancil ☎ 289 396666; www.quintadolagohotel.com 🕐 All year

Quinta dos Amigos (££)

Spend a week on a typical Portuguese farm and learn to ride or improve your horse-riding finesse. The Quinta dos Amigos is ideal for families with older children. There are good beaches near by, and the watersports, discos, restaurants and golf courses of Vale do Lobo and Quinta do Lago are 10 minutes' drive away. Qualified instructors organise rural rides or canters along the beach. The self-catering accommodation consists of brightly decorated apartments in converted farm buildings.

✉ Escanxinas, 8135 Almancil ☎ 289 395269 🕐 All year

Alte

Alte Hotel (££)

Many of the people who come here are walkers, taking advantage of the village's central location to explore the fascinating Barrocal countryside, with its limestone caves, cliffs and valleys and unspoiled

Portuguese way of life. Rooms are simple but comfortable, and facilities include tennis courts and a swimming pool, plus a restaurant specialising in fresh fish, game and rural Portuguese dishes such as pigs' trotters.

Montino, Alte, 8100 Loulé
289 478523 **All year**

Vale do Lobo

Le Meridien Dona Filipa (£££)

Part of the manicured and prestigious Vale do Lobo estate, the Dona Filipa enjoys a privileged position beside the Atlantic, a few feet from the beach and surrounded by golf courses – guests enjoy discounted green fees and an early start at the São Lourenço Club, rated one of the best in Europe. There are three floodlit tennis courts and a heated outdoor swimming pool to enjoy, as well as the tranquillity of this relatively small, elegant hotel. The two restaurants pride themselves on their wine lists.

Vale do Lobo, 8136 Almancil
289 394141; www.lemeridien-hotels.com
All year

Vilamoura

Tivoli Marinotel (£££)

This is a large hotel overlooking the marina at Vilamoura. The pleasures of the resort lie right on your doorstep, and there is a beach near by. Rooms are luxurious, and include a computer with Internet access, and the hotel offers a range of sports on site.

8125-901 **289 389988; www.nexus-pt.com/marinotel**
All year

Eastern Algarve

Monte Gordo

Hotel Navegadores (£££)

One of the largest hotels in Monte Gordo, the Navegadores sits 100m from the exceptional beach. The hotel is 1970s in style and rooms are simple, but there is a good-sized indoor pool, gym and spa on site.

Rua Gonçalo Velho, 8900
281 510860 **All year**

São Brás de Alportel

Pousada São Brás (££)

Set in the peaceful foothills of São Brás de Alportel, this state-run hotel, part of Portugal's *pousada* chain, was built in 1944 but has been modernised. The rooms are decorated in typical Algarvian style, and the facilities include a swimming pool and tennis court.

8150 São Brás de Alportel
01 848 9078; www.pousadas.pt **All year**

Vila Real de Santo António

Hotel Guadiana (£)

This grand, historic hotel is classed as a national monument, and its décor includes frescoed walls, elegant marble statues of langorous female nudes and delightfully decorated rooms. Some rooms look across the River Guadiana to Spain and the ferry to Ayamonte leaves from the opposite side of the road. Seville and Granada are within driving distance and the long, sandy beaches of Monte Gordo are only 5 minutes away.

Avenida da República 94, Vila Real de Santo António, 8900 Monte Gordo **281 511482**
All year

Gradings and Prices

Hotels in the Algarve are graded from 1 to 5 stars, but there is considerable variation between the cost of a 3-star hotel on the coast, for example, and one in a less tourist-visited inland town – prices drop rapidly once you move away from the coast. For rock-bottom prices, look out for the simple *pensão* or residential guest houses, often in town centres, offering clean, no-frills accommodation. Above this, a 3-star hotel will probably consist of a modern, purpose-built block, with clean and comfortable rooms and en suite bathrooms, a restaurant and small pool. Buildings with greater character may style themselves as an *estalagem* or *albergeria*, and anything styled as a *quinta* is probably a luxurious converted manor house, at the centre of its own expansive estate.

Antiques & Artesanato

Shop Opening Hours

Shops in the Algarve are generally open from Monday to Friday 9–1 and 3–7, and on Saturday 9–1. During the summer, many stay open through the siesta period, especially those in tourist resorts, and until 10PM at night, or later. Supermarkets in resorts open on Sundays and holidays. During the winter, opening hours are less predictable. Some shops catering exclusively for tourists close altogether from the beginning of November through to Easter.

Antiques

Faro

Vila Adentro Galleria

Six rooms full of antiques in the old town just north of the cathedral. Everything from inexpensive books, bottles, plates and postcards to medieval religious statuary and paintings.

✉ Rua do Castelo 21
Mon–Sun 10–8

Lagos

Casa do Papagaio

You cannot miss this shop as you walk down Rua 25 de Abril because of its live parrot, prominently positioned outside the door. Inside, the cramped store is packed with everything from junk to genuine antique statuary.

✉ Rua 25 de Abril
Mon–Fri 10–1, 3–7, Sat 10–1

São Brás Alportel

Dardevaia

An old town house filled with furniture, cookware and pottery.

✉ Rua Gago Coutinho 47
Mon–Fri 9–12:30, 3–7, Sat 9–1

Silves

Antiques Gallery

This is an upmarket antiques store in the square west of the cathedral selling ceramics, glass, jewellery and paintings, along with fine furniture.

✉ Largo D J Osório
Mon–Sun 10–8

Vilamoura

Seculo XIX

Interesting shop with cut glass, jewellery and china.

✉ Marina Plaza Summer 10–8; winter 10–1, 3–8

Artesanato

Artesanato shops specialise in typical Portuguese products. These include dolls made from hessian, woven baskets, cork products, place mats, coasters and floor mats, lace products such as tablecloths, decorative collars and pillow slips, woollen shawls and chunky sweaters, handmade rugs, brightly painted earthenware jars, copper lamps, almond confectionery, painted cockerels and models of traditional sailing vessels, called caravels, carved in wood. Many also sell ceramics – hand-painted plates, tiles and jugs – though it is more interesting to shop for these at the workshops where they are produced (► Ceramics 106).

Albufeira

O Pipote

Tiny shop selling quality ceramics, basketry and embroidery.

✉ Rua Joaquim Manuel Gouveia 15 Summer daily 10–8; winter Mon–Sat 10–1, 3–8

Alte

Café Regional

Café that doubles as a shop selling attractive hand-painted plates and basketry.

✉ Just south of the parish church, in Alte's main square
Mon–Sun 8–1, 3–7

Galerias Ivette

Painted plates and realistic silk flowers are among the best buys in a huge shop full of every kind of souvenir.

✉ Just southeast of the parish church, in Alte's main square Mon–Sun 8–1, 3–7

Alvor
Caleidoscopio
Cork products, including handbags and watch straps.
✉ Rua 25 de Abril 6
🕐 Mon–Sat 8–1, 3–7

Cabanas
O Vale
A shop/café selling garden pots and local products.
✉ Almargem, on the N125 north of Cabanas 🕐 9–8

Faro
Porta da Moura
Ceramics, textiles and toys.
✉ Rua do Repouso 5
🕐 Mon–Sun 10–8

Lagos
Poticho
Ceramics, basketwork and embroidery.
✉ Rua 25 de Abril 24 🕐 Daily 9–7. Closed Sun in winter

Loulé
Centro de Artesanato
Perhaps the best display in the Algarve: more unusual items include ornaments made from palm leaves and wood caravels.
✉ Rua da Barbacã
🕐 Mon–Sun 8–1, 3–7

O Arco
Next to an arch in the old town walls, selling hand-painted plates.
✉ Rua das Almadas
🕐 Mon–Sun 8–1, 3–7

Monchique
O Descansa Pernas
Cork, pottery, leather goods and ornaments.
✉ Estrada de Saboia
🕐 Mon–Sun 10–1, 3–8

O Poço
Cork products and hand-painted pottery.
✉ Estrada da Fóia
🕐 Mon–Sun 10–1, 3–8

Portimão
José Eliseu
Watch this artist creating products in stained glass.
✉ Vivenda Três Nações, Aldeia das Sobreiras ☎ 282 422364 to arrange a visit

O Aquário
Glass, ceramics, wicker and dolls, plus Atlantis Crystal and Vista Alegre porcelain.
✉ Praça da República
🕐 Summer Mon–Sat 9:30–7; winter Mon–Fri 9:30–1, 3–7, Sat 9:30–1

Querença
Afarrobinha
Barn-like shop selling handicrafts and local foods.
✉ Largo Igreja 🕐 Mon–Fri 10–1, 3–6, Sat 10–1

Sagres
Artesanato Algarvio
On the main road into Sagres, with fine *azulejos*, and other local products.
✉ N268 🕐 9–8

Silves
Estabelecimento D Sancho
Viennese-style coffee house with souvenir shop.
✉ Largo do Castelo
🕐 Mon–Sun 10–8

Tavira
Alart
Modern pottery and crafts.
✉ Rua de Caleria
🕐 Mon–Fri 10–1, 3–7, Sat 10–1

Vila Real de Santo António
Estabelecimentos Sol Dourado
Huge product range.
✉ Rua Dr Teófilo Braga
🕐 Mon–Fri 10–1, 3–8, Sat 10–1

The Cockerel of Barcelos
Souvenir shops throughout Portugal sell cockerels of all sizes, in many different colours and guises, and the Algarve is no exception. This national symbol stands for honesty and truthfulness. According to a popular folk story, the guest at a banquet in Barcelos was publicly accused of theft. Hauled before a judge, he was pronounced guilty and sentenced to hang. To prove his innocence, the condemned man pointed to a cockerel that was being served to the judge on a silver platter and declared that the bird would crow. To everyone's astonishment the bird stood up and duly crowed.

Basketry, Ceramics & Pottery

Basketry

Baskets make lightweight and inexpensive presents. Made all over the Algarve, and sold in *artesanato* shops, the capacious bags are derived from the sort that peasant farmers have developed over the centuries for carrying produce to and from the fields and markets – flexible shoulder bags and panniers made from straw or *esparto* grass.

A *cesteiro* (basket maker) can be found on the return leg of the Fonte de Benémola Walk (➤ 73). His prices are very low.

Basketry

Tavira

Artesanato Regional Bazar Tanger

Basket weavers can sometimes be seen at work here making bags, hats, toys, dolls, table mats and floor coverings.

Rua José Pires Padhina **Mon–Sat 10–1, 3–7. Closed Sun**

Casa do Artesanato de Tavira

A range of craft skills, from miniature boat-making to basketry and weaving.

Rua D Marcelino Franco 23

Ceramics and Pottery

Albufeira

Casa Tango

A good selection of pottery, as well as other crafts.

Trav Cândido dos Reis, 3–1 **289 587008**

Infante Dom Henrique

Specialises in fine earthenware.

40 Rua Cândido dos Rei **Mon–Sun 10–8**

Alte

Ceramica d'Alte

On the main road below the village centre, Ceramica d'Alte produces ceramics on site. Watch the potter and painter as you browse.

Estrada National 124 **10–1, 3–6**

Alvor

Artesanato Alexandre

Painted pottery and other souvenirs.

Rua Dr António José de Almeida **Mon–Sat 8–1, 3–7**

Lagos

O Caixote

Traditional pottery from all over Portugal, including replica chimneypots, mugs and painted plates and the ubiquitous pottery rooster (➤ 105).

Rua 25 de Abril **Mon–Sat 8–1, 3–7**

Loulé

Alegrete

Here you will find terracotta jars, garden ornaments and wood-fired cooking pots with an attractive patina.

Rua Miguel Bombarda 66–68 **Mon–Sun 8–1, 3–7**

Casa Louart

Some of the prettiest hand-painted pottery in town, with bold designs of fruit and flowers.

Rua Dom Paio Peres 19 **289 413794** **Mon–Sun 8–1, 3–7**

Porches

Olaria Algarve Pottery

Set in a shady Algarve mansion, Olaria produces patterned ceramics, and you can watch the artists at work.

N125, Porches **10–6**

Portimão

Casa Celiarte

Bright, hand-painted ceramics.

Rua 5 de Outubro **10–1, 3–6**

Tavira

Artesanato Regional Casa Matias

Traditional pottery, based in the market.

Mercado Ribeira, Rua do Cais **Mon–Sat 10–1, 3–7. Closed Sun**

Leatherware & Metalwork

Leatherware

Portuguese craftsmanship in leather is renowned throughout Europe. The Algarve has a number of shops selling beautifully made goods at good-value prices.

Algarvian leather workers also specialise in tooled leather, and there is a long tradition of saddle-making in the region.

Albufeira

Kitanda

Leather goods, including bags, purses, gloves and jackets.

Rua Alves Correia
9–1, 2–6 (till 8 in summer)

Faro

Oberon

Smart shoes, handbags and a range of accessories.

Rua de Santo António 67
Mon–Sun 10–8

Lagos

Crisbel

A comprehensive range of leather handbags, suitcases and purses.

Rua 25 de Abril 62
Mon–Fri 9–1, 2–6, Sat 9–1

Sirocco

Sirocco is on Rua Cândido dos Reis, one of the main shopping streets in Lagos, known for leather boutiques. The shop focuses on African crafts, including leather lamps and mirrors from Morocco.

Rua Cândido dos Reis 37

Loulé

Correaria Moderna

Watch saddles and harnesses being made and shop for leather belts, wallets, purses and handbags.

Rua da Barbacã
Mon–Sat 8–1, 3–7

Malas Vinhas

The leather goods on sale here include sandals, boots and handbags.

Rua 5 de Outubro 55
Mon–Sat 8–1, 3–7. Closed Sun

Portimão

Chic Shoes

This shop specialises in handmade leather boots and shoes.

Rua Direita
Mon–Sat 10–1, 3–8

Leather Factory

The Leather Factory sells everything from shoes and belts to skirts and waistcoats – take your pick.

Rua Dr J V Mealha
Mon–Sat 10–1, 3–8

Metalwork

Loulé

Barracha

Here you will find *cataplanas* and cooking pots for authentic Algarve cooking, reproduction stills, lighting and fireside ornaments in copper, wrought iron and brass.

Rua José Fernando Guerreiro (to the south of the market) **Mon–Sat 8–1, 3–7. Closed Sun**

Caldeiraria Louletana

This workshop specialises in handmade brass and copper goods, which you can watch being made.

Rua da Barbacã
Mon–Sat 8–1, 3–7. Closed Sun

Algarvian Pottery

Ceramic techniques were introduced to the Algarve by the Moors and the tradition has never died. Among the region's products are terracotta pots for use in the garden, and hand-painted jugs, plates and bowls, decorated with brightly coloured fruit and flower motifs. Also popular are hand-painted cockerels (*gallos*) in every size and shape, and miniature versions of the ornate Algarvian chimneys that are seen on older houses throughout the region. In addition, *azulejos* are still made – thick, chunky irregular tiles with blue and white or polychrome painted decorations. Genuine antique *azulejos* are sold singly and are expensive, but modern tiles are sold in sets for use as floor or wall decorations.

Markets

Loulé's Market

If you want the best combination of permanent market and street market, go to Loulé on a Saturday. Head for the Moorish-style building in Avenida José da Costa Mealha. Here, every street in the vicinity of the covered market has its smallholders, from farmers with sacks of grain and animal feed to souvenir stalls piled with painted cockerels and plates. For gourmets, there is a delightful range of home-produced food on sale, including herb-marinated olives, dried figs, almond-based sweets, bundles of dried spices, sweet cheeses, hams and spicy sausages.

Permanent Markets

Every town of any size has a permanent covered market, which opens every day except Sunday from 6:30AM and which stays open until around 1PM, though the later you arrive, the less choice there will be. Markets are being upgraded to comply with EU hygiene standards, but this has been achieved without destroying their character.

There are usually separate areas for fish and for fruit and vegetables, and some have butcher's shops in separate premises around the perimeter of the hall. Larger markets also have stalls selling delicious home-baked bread, mountain-cured ham and local sheep's-milk cheeses. Farmers sometimes set up *ad hoc* stalls in the streets around the entrance to the market, selling anything from a rabbit or a chicken to bunches of herbs or jars of honey. You may also find second-hand clothes and bric-a-brac.

Four of the best produce markets are:

Lagos

The market is in temporary accommodation until 2003 to allow for renovation of the old market building on Rua das Portes de Portugal.

Rua Vasco de Gama
Mon–Sat 8–1

Loulé

Set in a striking, tiled, Moorish-style building, dating from the 1930s, and with the most varied range of stalls of any market in the Algarve.

Praça da República
Mon–Sat 8–1

Olhão

The biggest and best in the region – two adjacent halls built in Moorish style, with fish and shellfish for sale in one and fruit and vegetables in the other.

Avenida 5 de Outubro
Mon–Sat 8–1

Silves

Everything under one roof, including delicious bread baked in a wood-fired oven.

Rua J Estevão
Mon–Sat 8–1

Street Markets

Itinerant merchants travel from town to town setting up stalls at what are sometimes called 'gypsy markets' or 'country markets'. In addition, some towns have a 'Saturday market', which centres around the covered market, but attracts many additional stallholders in the surrounding streets. The stalls sell literally everything you could ever want.

Main markets:

Albufeira: 1st and 3rd Tuesday of the month (in Orada to the west of the town).
Almancil: 4th Sunday of the month.
Alvor: 2nd Tuesday of the month.
Lagos: 1st Saturday of the month.
Quarteira: every Wednesday.
Loulé: every Saturday.
Monchique: 2nd Friday of the month.
Portimão: 1st Monday of the month (next to the station).
Sagres: 1st Friday of the month (opposite the post office).
Silves, Tavira: 3rd Monday of the month.

Shopping Malls & Miscellaneous

Shopping Malls

In recent years a number of American-style shopping malls have sprung up in the Algarve. Here is a selection:

Albufeira

AlgarveShopping

This is the largest and most modern shopping centre along the coast, with 133 shops and a nine-screen cinema complex.

On the N125, west of Albufeira **10AM–11PM**

Faro

Faro Shopping Center

This shopping centre, on the outskirts of Faro, has more than 60 shops, three cinemas, a hypermarket and a restaurant. There is nothing particularly Portuguese about it, and prices tend to be higher than in town, but it is handy if you want the convenience of everything under one roof.

On the N125, Sítio das Figuras

Quinta do Lago

Quinta Shopping

A stylish low-rise mall of 63 upmarket shops, restaurants and beauty salons, around a central plaza.

Quinta do Lago **289 398247** **10–8**

Miscellaneous

Lagos

Triarte

Designer jewellery, blown glass and hand-painted silk in this small shop near the slave market. The shop will also make goods to order.

Rua da Vedoria
9–7

Almancil

Florida Golf

Everything for the golf fanatic, including golf-themed shoes, bags, accessories, books and gifts.

Vale de Éguas, N125
Mon–Sat 8–1, 3–7

Griffin Bookshop

The Algarve's best-stocked English-language bookshop, with a good range of fiction and non-fiction titles for children and adults, plus second-hand books.

Rua 5 de Outubro 206-A
289 393904 **Mon–Sat 8–1, 3–7**

Ipê Amarelo

Art and crafts from Brazil in this funky shop on Amancil's main street.

Rua Duarte Pacheco 82
Mon–Fri 9–1, 2–6, Sat 9–1

Faro

António Zucannel

Designer fashions for women: Versace, Polo, etc.

Rua de Santo António 48
Mon–Fri 10–1, 3–7, Sat 10–1

Palloram

Upmarket men's fashions.

Rua de Santo António 53
Mon–Fri 10–1, 3–7, Sat 10–1

Monte Gordo

Gemas do Mundo

Crystals, semi-precious stones and fossils from around the world.

Rua Gil Eanes 29a
9–8

Olhão

A Margerida

Soft furnishings and picture frames.

Rua do Comércio
Mon–Fri 10–1, 3–7, Sat 10–1

Wines and Spirits

Just head for any supermarket in the Algarve to find a comprehensive stock of local products. Most local wines are best drunk in the Algarve, but one or two travel well: look for the names Arade or Lagoa on the label. You might also like to buy classic Portuguese wines from beyond the Algarve, such as Dão, *vinho verde* or port. Local liqueurs include distilled arbutus berries (*medronho*) and *amêndoa amarga*, a delicious almond-based liqueur.

Children's Attractions

Watersports
Think twice before allowing your children to ride on water inflatables, such as ringos and bananas, which are pulled along at high speed behind a powerboat. Though popular and heavily promoted, the bumpy ride has caused a number of injuries, and nervous children are easily frightened. Stick with the more sedate pedalos instead.

Theme Parks and Water Parks

The Algarve has four large water parks, and although half-day tickets are available, it is easy and enjoyable to make them the focus of a whole day.

Facilities are graded so that children of all ages will find something to thrill and challenge them, from junior slides and pools for younger children to 'corkscrew slides' and 'black holes' for the older ones.

Fully qualified lifeguards are on hand to ensure safety, and there are snack bars and restaurants for when you need a break from the action.

Alcantarilha

The Big One

Exciting attractions, with names like 'Raging Rapids', 'Flying Carpets' and 'Crazy Leap', make this a must for the daring. The park has the longest speed slide in the Algarve.

On the N125 main highway at Alcantarilha ☎ 282 322827; www.bigone-waterpark.com Daily 10–6. Closed Nov–Easter

Estômbar

Slide and Splash

Experience the exciting 'Black Hole' whirlpool at this popular park. Facilities include shops, bars and a restaurant. Slide and Splash runs buses during the summer, collecting customers from pick-up points in the main coastal resorts.

Just off the N125, at Vale de Deus, near Estômbar ☎ 282 341685 Daily 10–6. Closed Nov–Easter

Guia

Zoomarine

One ticket provides entry to the marine zoo and water park. Shows featuring dolphins, seals and parrots are staged through the day, and other attractions include an aquarium, cinema, sea museum, funfair, swimming pools with slides and whirlpools, and restaurants.

On the N125 at the Guia junction, near Albufeira ☎ 289 560300; www.zoomarine.com Daily 10–6. Closed Nov–Easter

Quarteira

Atlantic Park

Thrilling slides for the energetic, with lots of long water slides and tunnels.

On the N125 at Quatro Estradas, near Quarteira ☎ 289 397282 Daily 9–6. Closed Nov–Easter

Trains, Boat Trips and Jeep Safaris

The Algarve railway travels from Vila Real de Santo António to Lagos, at a sedate speed. Children may enjoy a ride, with its interesting coastal scenery.

In Praia da Rocha, the Rocha Express road train runs along the promenade in summer, leaving Miradouro at half-hourly intervals from 10–12:30 and 3–6:30, calling at Fortaleza, Praia do Vau and Rotunda Presidente. Buy your tickets on board.

Jeep safaris explore some of the lesser-known parts of the Algarve, travelling on unsurfaced roads.

Albufeira

Zebra Safari

The Strip ☎ 289 583300; www.zebrasafari.com

Lagos and Portimão
Dolphin Safari

Travel in high-speed rigid inflatable boats (RIBs) to catch sight of these gentle marine creatures.

Marina de Lagos and Marina de Portimão 282 792586 Trips daily

Praia da Rocha
Mount Safari

Rua Eng. José Bivar
282 420800

Mini-golf

Albufeira
Krazy World

Mini-golf, quad-bike racing and an exotic animal farm in tropical gardens.

Signposted from the N125 at Guia 282 574134
10–7:30

Vilamoura
Roma Golf Park

Two mini-golf courses with children's activities and snack bar.

Rua dos Marmeleiros, s/n Vilamoura 289 300800
10–7:30

Horse Riding

The Algarve has numerous stables offering riding lessons for everyone from adults to infants and from total beginners to seasoned hackers, usually with English-speaking instructors. Lessons can be booked by the hour, or you can go trekking through glorious countryside or cantering along the beach on half- or full-day trips.

Since most of the stables are based in the countryside, they will send transport to meet you, and will provide picnic food or refreshments for longer outings.

Centro de Equitação Quinta das Oliveiras

Estrada Nacional N125, Tavira
281 322107

Centro Hipico da Penina

Portimão
282 415415

Tiffany's Riding Centre

Lagos
282 96444

Vale Navio

Albufeira
289 542870

Miscellaneous

Almancil
Almancil Karting

Karting circuit designed as a small replica of the Brazilian Grand Prix track and inaugurated by the late Ayrton Senna. Separate children's track.

Sítio de Pereiras
089 399899; www.mundokarting.pt
Summer daily 9–8; winter daily 9–4

Barão de São João
Lagos Zoological Park

Barão de São João, north-west of Lagos, is home to one of the Algarve's newest attractions, Lagos Zoological Park. Three hectares of land have been transformed into various habitats, home to exotic birds, monkeys, emus and wallabies, to name but a few. There are refreshment facilities, as well as an area where children can interact with the animals.

Sítio do Medronhal, Barão de São João 282 688236
May–Sep daily 10–7; Oct–Apr daily 10–5
Expensive

Indulgence

Fair-haired children may get fed up of being patted on the head or shoulders by strangers, but it is a fact of life that the Portuguese regard them as especially fortunate, so any would-be lottery-prize winner will want a bit of your child's luck. No harm is meant – the Portuguese love children. In restaurants, children are welcomed and indulged, and parents can bask in the extra attention that well-behaved families get wherever they go.

Fado & Cinemas

Casinos

Casinos offer free entry to slot machines and video games. Proof of age must be provided to gain entry to the gaming machines, and there may be a charge. Visitors must be smartly dressed. Some casinos offer a nightly dinner and floorshow.

Monte Gordo
✉ Avenida Marginal
☎ 081 512224

Praia da Rocha
✉ Hotel Casino Algarve
☎ 082 415001

Vilamoura
✉ Praia da Marina
☎ 089 302999

Fado

Fado is unique to Portugal; like the blues, it is claimed to have its origins in African slave music, but the music developed its present form in mid-19th-century Lisbon. *Fado* means 'fate', and the lyrics of each three-minute song express the sadness and yearning occasioned by lost or unrequited love or the vicissitudes of life.

The *fadista*, or singer, traditionally wears black. The accompaniment is provided by two musicians, one of whom plays the pear-shaped *quitarra portuguesa* (a 12-stringed Portuguese guitar), while the other provides the bass line on a Spanish guitar.

Alvor

Hotel Delphim
Holds *fado* evenings one week, folk evenings the next.
✉ **Praia dos Três Irmãos**
☎ **282 458901**

Almancil

Quinta do Lago
✉ **Hotel Quinta do Lago, Quinta do Lago**
☎ **289 350350** 🕐 ***Fado* performances Thu**

Lagos

Restaurante A Muralha
✉ **15 Rua da Atalaia**
☎ **282 763659** 🕐 **Tue–Sun**

Monte Gordo

Hotel Navegadores
✉ **Rua Gonçalo Velho**
☎ **281 512490**
🕐 ***Fado* performances Wed**

Porches

Restaurante Porches Velho
✉ **N 125 main highway at Porches, near Lagoa**
☎ **282 381692**
🕐 **Performances Fri, Sat, 9PM**

Portimão

Restaurante A Vela
✉ **97-r/c Dr Manuel Alma**
☎ **282 414016**
🕐 **Performances Thu, Sat**

Silves

Quinta Pomona
✉ **26-r/c 5 Outubro**
☎ **282 416350**
🕐 **Performances Wed, Thu 8PM**

Vale do Lobo

Le Meridien Dona Filipe Hotel
✉ **Vale do Lobo, 8136 Almancil**
☎ **289 394141**
🕐 ***Fado* performances Mon; folk song and dance Wed**

Cinemas

Many of the Algarve's multi-screen cinemas are in shopping complexes.
Films are shown in their original language, usually English.
Film buffs may be interested in the Algarve's International Film Festival in May, when Portuguese and foreign films are shown at cinemas in Alvor, Lagoa, Lagos and Loulé, in their original language; ☎ 01 851 3615 for further details.

Albufeira

AlgarveShopping
✉ **On the N125, west of Albufeira**
☎ **289 560350**

Faro

Faro Shopping Center
✉ **On the N125, Sítio das Figuras**
☎ **289 806547**

Portimão

Modelo de Portimão (shopping centre)
✉ **Quinta da Malata, Lote 1**
☎ **282 415272**

Boat Trips, Fishing & Watersports

Boat Trips and Fishing

Lagos

Lagos Kayak Centre

Take part in guided freshwater kayak trips (along the river, not on the sea) in modern kayaks.

Motel Âncora, Estrada do Porto do Mós

282 782718; www.blue-ocean-divers.de

Pescamar

Pescamar runs big-game fishing trips, daily.

Lagos Marina

966 193431

Bom Dia

The Bom Dia company specialises in trips to explore the marine caves of the nearby coastline. Visitors travel along the coast in a tall-masted sailing ship, using smaller boats to explore the marine grottoes.

Lagos marina

282 764670

Sagres

Coastal tours

Explore the awe-inspiring cliffs of Fim do Mundo (World's End) and the windswept Costa Vicentina. There are also three-hour fishing trips, for first-timers and experienced anglers. If you want bigger challenges, shark-fishing trips depart at 8AM Tuesday and Thursday (half-day excursions) and Saturday (full day).

Turinfo, Praça de Republica

282 620003

Vilamoura

Cruzeiros da Olva

Fishing and pleasure trips.

Marina da Vilamoura

289 315638

River Cruises

If you are prone to sea-sickness but still fancy a boat trip, try a river cruise, where the water is gentler.

Monte Gordo

River Guadiana Cruise

Rua Tristao vaz Teixeira

281 510201

Portimão

Arade River Cruise

Leãozinho Arade River Cruises, Portimão harbour

282 415156

Vila Real de Santa António

Tourismar

Avenida da Republica

968 066549

Watersports

Carvoeiro

Divers Cove Portugal

Training, certification and accompanied dives.

Quinta do Paraíso, Praia de Carvoeiro 282 356594; www.diverscove.de

Lagos

Blue Ocean Divers

Great trips for qualified divers, as well as equipment hire and training to advanced level.

Motel Âncora, Estrada do Porto do Mós 282 782718; www.blue-ocean-divers.de

Vilamoura

Marina Watersports

If you want to get above the waves rather than on or beneath them, try one of the parascending cruises that depart at 10, 12, 4 and 6 daily. The parachutes are controlled by a hydraulic winch that gives a gentle take-off and landing.

Marina da Vilamoura

289 388149

Helicopter Flights

If you would rather have a bird's-eye view of the coastline, splash out on a sightseeing helicopter flight. Contact Sky Zone at the Aerodrome Municipal de Portimão, Montes de Alvor, 8500-059, Alvor 282 459926; www.skyzone.pt

Keeping Fit

Bicycle Hire
Hiring a bicycle is a great way to explore the Algarve. Many local councils in the region have created cycle lanes and marked routes along the coast and through the countryside. Bicycles can be rented from:

Algarve2Bike
✉ Largo do Mercado, Albufeira
☎ 289 585886

Sport Nautica
✉ Rua Jacques Pessoa 26, Tavira
☎ 281 324371

Vilar du Golfe
✉ Quinta do Lago
☎ 289 352000

Sports Facilities

Praia da Luz

The facilities at the Luz Bay and Ocean clubs are open to non-residents and include swimming pools, saunas, a Turkish bath, gym, mini-golf, tennis and squash courts.
✉ **Avenida Pescadores, Praia da Luz, 8600 Lagos**
☎ **282 789472**

Carvoeiro

The Rocha Brava Tennis Club is open to visitors, who are encouraged to use the facilities and join in tournaments. Equipment hire and coaches available.
✉ **Rocha Brava, Praia do Carvoeiro** ☎ **282 358856**

Vale do Lobo

Barringtons
Apart from the well-known golf academy, with its floodlit driving range and instruction, this complex includes squash courts, a cricket pitch with nets, a fitness centre, sauna, Turkish bath and jacuzzi, indoor and outdoor swimming pools and a snooker room.
✉ **Vale do Lobo**
☎ **289 396622; www.barringtons-pt.com**

Vilamoura

Rock Garden
This is one of the Algarve's best-equipped sports centres, offering indoor and outdoor swimming pools, tennis and squash courts. Also available are a Turkish bath, snooker tables, table tennis, darts, a gym and a fitness suite.
✉ **Aldeia do Campo**
☎ **289 322740**

Vilamoura Tennis Centre
The Vilamoura Tennis Club, just off the resort's marina, has 12 courts. After your match, you can recharge your batteries in the club's restaurant and bar. Equipment hire and individual or group tuition is available.
✉ **Vilamoura**
☎ **289 310169**

Walking Tours

For gentle exercise of the body (and mind), some local councils in the Algarve organise walking tours of their major towns. Here is a selection:

Albufeira

Tours of the Archaeological Museum and the medieval town centre (➤ 66).
✉ **Cultural department of the Town Council, Rua Centenario Velha**
☎ **289 588957**

Aljezur

Tours of the historic centre (➤ 35).
✉ **Town Council, Rua do Republica**
☎ **282 998102**

Faro

Tours of the Algarvian capital's historic centre (➤ 62–65).
✉ **The Archaeology Museum, Largo Dom Afonso III**
☎ **289 897400**

Tavira

Choose from three different tour routes, each starting at the tourist office, on Rua da Galeria (➤ 78–79).
✉ **(For information) Tavira Development Agency, Rua da Liberdade**
☎ **281 321946**

Golf

The Algarve is one of Europe's most popular destinations for golfing holidays, with many specialist tour operators. Large numbers of visitors come here for no other reason than to spend a week perfecting their skills. The region has 24 courses, and some of them are renowned throughout the world for their challenging terrain and beautiful surroundings. The following courses are among those highly rated by golfers:

Alvor

Alto Golf

This cliff-top course enjoys superb views of the sea and the Serra de Monchique mountains. Designed by Sir Henry Cotton, the challenging course is famous for its 16th hole, one of the longest in Europe. There is also a golf school with practice bunker and putting green. 18 holes, par 72.

✉ Quinta do Alto do Poço, Alvor ☎ 282 460870

Carvoeiro

Pestana Golf

The base for the David Leadbetter Golf Academy, with two scenic 18-hole courses.

✉ Carvoeiro ☎ 282 340900

Vale de Milho

Nine-hole, par-27 course, with challenging water hazards.

✉ Apartado 273, Carvoeiro
☎ 282 358502

Vale da Pinta

New 18-hole course, built around an ancient olive grove.

✉ Carvoeiro ☎ 282 340900

Vale do Lobo

Pinheiros Altos

This par-72, 18-hole course begins in attractive pine woods, while the back nine holes run alongside the Ria Formosa Nature Reserve.

✉ Quinta do Lago
☎ 289 359910

Quinta do Lago

Designed by Henry Cotton, the two 18-hole, par-72 courses feature lakes and challenging bunkers. Rated one of the best golf complexes in Europe, the Portuguese Open and other international tournaments are regularly hosted here.

✉ Quinta do Lago
☎ 289 396141

San Lorenzo

To play this 27-hole course (with three 9-hole loops) you must be a guest at the luxurious Dona Filipa (▶ 103) or Penina hotels. Keen golfers consider the expense worthwhile for the chance to play a golf course that is currently rated number two in Europe, with its famous 7th hole (on the yellow loop) straddling two ravines.

✉ Quinta do Lago
☎ 289 396522

Vilamoura

The Vilamoura estate, west of Faro, has three courses designed for a range of abilities, from the testing Vilamoura I to the 27-hole Vilamoura III course with three 9-hole combinations, set among lakes.

✉ Vilamoura ☎ Old Course 289 310341; Pinhal 289 310390; Laguna 289 310180

Remember

Almost all golf courses in the Algarve require a handicap certificate and most have a dress code. Remember to check your tee-off time when booking.

What's on When

Information

Pick up *Algarve Events* from the airport as you arrive or from tourist information centres. The brochure lists forthcoming cultural events in the region for the month ahead.

February

Carnival (weekend preceding Shrove Tuesday): steel barriers go up all over the Algarve on the Saturday before Shrove Tuesday, sealing off town centres from traffic so that the weekend's carnival can proceed without interruption. Typically, Saturday sees local children take part in a costume parade through the streets, while the irreverent 'satirical parade' takes place the following day. Loulé Carnival has the biggest and best procession, with colourful floats, bands and scantily clad dancers. Be warned, though, that water bombs, eggs, flour and other substances can be hurled at spectators during this and other carnival parades, so don't wear your best clothes.

April

Holy Week (especially Palm Sunday, Good Friday and Easter Saturday): religious processions in the streets of many towns, when actors re-enact scenes from the Passion and Crucifixion of Christ.

May

May Day Folk Festival (1st May): traditional singing and folk dancing, with food and drink on sale in Alcoutim, Albufeira, Alte and Monchique.

June/July

International Music Festival: sponsored by the Gulbenkian Foundation, this is the biggest arts festival in the Algarve, with top international artists performing in a number of centres, including Albufeira and Silves.

July

Algarve Jazz Festival (all month): local and international musicians come together for this celebration.
Alcoutim Handicraft Festival (2nd or 3rd week): see the best of the region's crafts as stalls line the streets.
Silves Beer Festival (all month): Silves Castle is taken over by brass bands and folk dancers in this celebration of Portuguese and international beers.
Feira do Carmo: Faro's own handicraft festival.

August

Fatacil (3rd week): Lagoa's country fair is a showcase for local agriculture, industry and commerce, with live bands and food and wine tastings.
Summer in Tavira: *fado*, folk and classical music, plus folk dancing in the open air in the city's parks and gardens.
Fish Festival (11 Aug): Cabanas celebrates the fruits of the sea with a market, folk music, dancing and *fado* music.
Banho de 29 (29 Aug): fireworks and live music to celebrate the end of the holiday season in Lagos.

September

National Folklore Festival (1st week): Portuguese folk music and dancing troupes come from as far away as Brazil and Madeira.
Lagoa Wine Festival (2nd week): tastings to promote local vintages.
Nossa Senhora das Dores (3rd week): country fair food stalls, fairground attractions and folk concerts, starting in Monte Gordo and moving on to Tavira.

Practical Matters

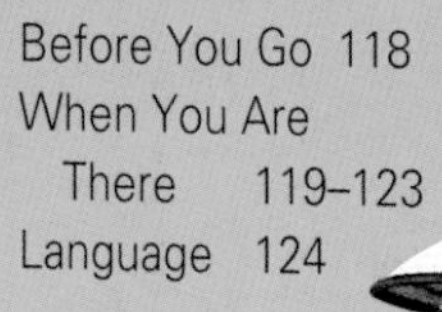

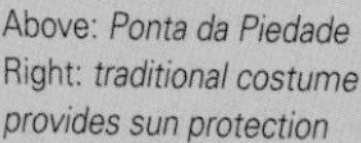

Above: *Ponta da Piedade*
Right: *traditional costume provides sun protection*

TIME DIFFERENCES

GMT
12 noon

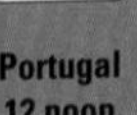

Portugal
12 noon

Germany
1PM

USA (NY)
7AM

Netherlands
1PM

Spain
1PM

BEFORE YOU GO

WHAT YOU NEED

● Required
○ Suggested
▲ Not required

	UK	Germany	USA	Netherlands	Spain
Passport/National Identity Card	●	●	●	●	●
Visa	▲	▲	▲	▲	▲
Onward or Return Ticket	○	○	○	○	○
Health Inoculations	▲	▲	▲	▲	▲
Health Documentation (➤ 123, Health)	○	○	○	○	○
Travel Insurance	○	○	○	○	○
Driving Licence (National)	●	●	●	●	●
Car Insurance Certificate (if own car)	●	●	●	●	●
Car registration document (if own car)	●	●	●	●	●

WHEN TO GO

Faro

High season

Low season

15°C	16°C	18°C	21°C	24°C	30°C	35°C	37°C	33°C	28°C	19°C	17°C
JAN	FEB	MAR	APR	MAY	JUN	JUL	AUG	SEP	OCT	NOV	DEC

Sun

Sunshine and showers

TOURIST OFFICES

In the UK
Portuguese National Tourist Office
22–25A Sackville Street
London W1X 1DE
☎ 020 7494 5725
Fax: 020 7494 1868;
www.rtalgarve.pt

In the USA
Portuguese National Tourist Office
590 Fifth Avenue, 4th Floor
New York
NY 10036
☎ 212/354 4403
Fax: 212/764 6137

POLICE 112

FIRE 112

AMBULANCE 112

WHEN YOU ARE THERE

ARRIVING

It is possible to drive to the Algarve from all parts of continental Europe, but most visitors arrive by air. Faro airport (☎ 289 800800) is served by scheduled and charter flights from most European airports. Because of the region's popularity as a winter destination, seats on direct flights get booked up well in advance and you might have to fly via Lisbon and drive. TAP Air Portugal is the national airline (in Faro ☎ 0808 213141)

Faro Airport
Kilometres to city centre

4 kilometres

Journey times

 N/A

 15 minutes

10 minutes

MONEY

The euro (€) is the official currency of Portugal. Euro banknotes and coins were introduced in January 2002. Banknotes are in denominations of 5, 10, 20, 50, 100, 200 and 500 euros; coins are in denominations of 1, 2, 5, 10, 20 and 50 cents, and 1 and 2 euros.
Euro traveller's cheques are widely accepted, as are major credit cards, although cash can be more useful in the countryside. Credit and debit cards can also be used for withdrawing euro notes from automatic teller machines (ATMs). Banks can be found in most towns, although they do not necessarily offer the best deal for changing money when charges are taken into account. Portugal's former currency, the *escudo*, went out of circulation in early 2002.

TIME

The Algarve observes Greenwich Mean Time during the winter months; during the summer, from late March to late October, the time is GMT plus one hour.

CUSTOMS

YES
From another EU country for personal use (guidelines):
800 cigarettes, 200 cigars, 1 kilogram of tobacco
10 litres of spirits (over 22%)
20 litres of aperitifs
90 litres of wine, of which 60 litres can be sparkling wine
110 litres of beer

From a non-EU country for your personal use, the allowances are:
200 cigarettes OR
50 cigars OR 20 grams of tobacco
1 litre of spirits (over 22%)
2 litres of intermediary products (e.g. sherry) and sparkling wine
2 litres of still wine
50 grams of perfume
0.25 litres of eau de toilette
The value limit for goods is 175 euros

Travellers under 17 years of age are not entitled to the tobacco and alcohol allowances

NO

Drugs, firearms, ammunition, offensive weapons, obscene material, unlicensed animals.

EMBASSIES AND CONSULATES

UK
082 417800

Germany
089 803148

USA
01 727 3300 (Lisbon)

Netherlands
089 20903

Spain
081 544888

WHEN YOU ARE THERE

TOURIST OFFICES

Algarve Tourism Regional Office

- Avenida 5 de Outubro 18
  8000 Faro
  ☎ 289 800400
  Fax: 289 800489

Local Offices

- Albufeira
  Rua 5 de Outobro 18
  ☎ 289 585279
- Faro
  Rua da Misericórdia 8–11
  ☎ 289 803604
- Lagos
  Rua Vasco da Gama, São João
  ☎ 282 763031
- Loulé
  Edifício do Castelo
  ☎ 289 463900
- Monchique
  Largo dos Chorões
  ☎ 282 911189
- Monte Gordo
  Avenida Marginal
  ☎ 281 544495
- Olhão
  Largo Sebastiano M Mestre
  ☎ 289 713936
- Portimão
  Avenida Zeca Afonso
  ☎ 282 416550
- Silves
  Rua 25 de Abril
  ☎ 282 442255
- Tavira
  Rua da Galeria 9
  ☎ 281 322511

NATIONAL HOLIDAYS

J	F	M	A	M	J	J	A	S	O	N	D
1	(2)	(2)	1(2)	1	1(1)		1		1	1	4

1 Jan	New Year
Feb (dates vary)	Shrove Tuesday and Ash Wednesday
Mar/Apr	Good Friday
Mar/Apr	Easter Monday
25 Apr	Day of the Revolution
1 May	Labour Day
Jun (date varies)	Corpus Christi
10 Jun	National Day
15 Aug	Feast of the Assumption
5 Oct	Republic Day
1 Nov	All Saints' Day
1 Dec	Restoration of Independence Day
8 Dec	Feast of the Immaculate Conception
25 Dec	Christmas Day
26 Dec	St Stephen's Day

OPENING HOURS

○ Shops ● Main Post Offices
● Offices ● Museums/Monuments
● Banks ● Pharmacies

8AM 9AM 10AM NOON 1PM 2PM 4PM 5PM 7PM

☐ Day ☐ Midday
☐ Evening

Shops catering to tourists open all day in the high season, until 9 or 10 in the evening, including Sundays and public holidays.
Larger stores and supermarkets increasingly ignore the lunch break and are open continuously from 9 to 7, with some supermarkets staying open until 10 (until 5 on Sundays).
Pharmacies open late on a duty rota (posted on pharmacy doors). Times of museum and church opening vary greatly – see individual museums for details.

PUBLIC TRANSPORT

Trains The Algarve railway line follows the south coast from Lagos in the west to Vila Real de Santo António in the east. Although the line is not much more than 130km in length, it can take up to 4½ hours to travel from one end to the other. Stations can be 6km or more from the towns that they serve, so check the map before deciding to use the train. It is cheap, however, and provides views of some fine coastal scenery. Tourist offices have timetables, and tickets should be bought before you get on the train, or else you risk a fine.

Buses Modern express bus services link most towns in the Algarve. Services are provided by a number of companies. EVA is the biggest, and it sells a useful Passe Turístico (Tourist Pass), which allows unlimited use of the network for three or seven days. Bus routes principally follow the main roads, and so are not a reliable way of exploring the more remote countryside. Timetables and route maps are available from tourist offices and main bus stations (*terminal rodoviário*). Have plenty of small change ready when boarding.

Ferries Although most people now travel from Portugal to Spain along the motorway bridge that links the two countries across the Guadiana, ferries do still operate. The car and passenger ferry from Vila Real to Ayamonte departs at 40-minute intervals throughout the day, and fishermen ferry passengers from Alcoutim to San Lúcar on demand. Ferry services also take visitors to the barrier islands in the Ria Formosa Nature Reserve during the summer months, departing from Tavira and Olhão at regular intervals during the day.

CAR RENTAL

The major car rental firms are represented in the Algarve, as well as several local companies who offer slightly cheaper rates. All rental firms send a courtesy bus to meet you at the airport on arrival, transporting you to their depot on the Faro airport road; alternatively, they will deliver the car to your hotel or villa.

TAXIS

In towns, it is usual to hire taxis from a rank. They may stop if flagged down, especially in the countryside. Rates for some journeys are fixed. Short journeys across town should be metered. For longer journeys, you can negotiate an hourly rate. Try to find a driver who speaks your language and who has a modern well-maintained car.

DRIVING

Speed limit on motorways:
120kph

Speed limit on main roads:
90kph

Speed limit on urban roads:
60 or **40kph**

Seat belts must be worn in front seats at all times and rear seats where fitted.

Random breath testing is carried out.

Petrol (*gasolina*) comes in two grades: lead-free (*sem chumbo*) and 4-star (*super*). Diesel (*gasóleo*) is also available. Most villages and towns have a petrol station, and they are generally open from 8 to 8.

All the car rental companies in the Algarve run their own breakdown and rescue services, details of which will be given to you when you rent your car. Main highways have orange SOS telephones for use in an emergency. Members of motoring organisations such as the AA and RAC can use the services of the ACP (Automóvel Clube de Portugal) ☎ 089 805753.

Random roadside police checks can impose heavy fines on motorists who are not carrying proof of insurance, rental documents, driving licence and passport.

0 1 2 3 4 5 6 7 8
CENTIMETRES
INCHES
0 1 2 3

PERSONAL SAFETY

Theft from cars and other petty crime is increasingly a problem. If you are the victim of theft, get help from a hotel or holiday representative because they know the correct procedures and can deal with the bureaucracy.
To make an insurance claim you must report thefts to the local police station and get a copy of the written statement.

- Leave your valuables in the hotel safe.
- Don't leave valuables in cars.
- Don't leave unattended valuables on the beach or poolside.
- Beware of pickpockets.

National Police assistance:
☎ **112 from any call box**

TELEPHONES

Telephones are found in many cafés, and there are booths in every town or village. Some take only phonecards, for 50 or 120 units, which can be bought from newsagents and cafés. A 50-unit card will give you about 5 minutes of overseas calls.
To call the Algarve from the UK, dial 00 351 (the international code for Portugal), then the area code (282, 289 or 281). Within the Algarve you only need the five- or six-digit number if you are dialling another number with the same area code: otherwise you need to dial the area code as well.

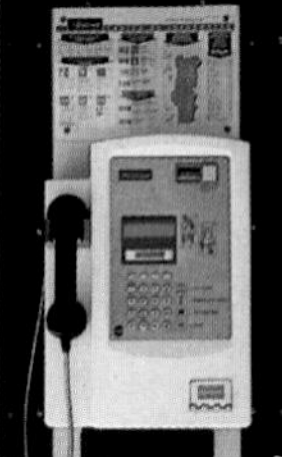

International Dialling Codes	
From the Algarve to:	
UK:	**00 44**
Germany:	**00 49**
USA & Canada:	**00 1**
Netherlands:	**00 31**
Spain:	**00 34**

POST

Post offices (*correios*) are found in main towns. In Faro, the most central post office is on Largo do Carmo, and post restante services are available here, and at all main post offices. Stamps can be bought from newsagents and hotel kiosks. Open: main office Mon–Fri 8:30 or 9–6, Sat 9–12:30. Smaller offices close 12:30–2:30.

ELECTRICITY

The power supply in Portugal is: 220 volts AC.
Sockets take two-pronged continental plugs, so an adaptor is needed for non-continental appliances, and a transformer for devices operating on 100–120 volts.

TIPS/GRATUITIES

Yes ✓ No ✕		
Restaurants (service included)	✓	10%
Bar service	✓	small change
Taxis	✓	10%
Tour guides	✕	
Porters	✓	€1
Chambermaids	✕	
Hairdressers	✓	10%
Cloakroom attendants	✓	small change
Toilets	✕	

What to photograph: the Algarve's wild coastline, wind-eroded sandstone cliffs, markets, flowers, traditional costumes, donkey carts and ploughs drawn by horse or mule.
Best time to photograph: the light is best before 10AM; after this the intensity of the sun can bleach out details. Sunsets can be spectacular in the west.
Buying film: most hotels have shops selling film and batteries, and there is usually at least one specialist photo shop in every town, selling film and offering processing services, .

HEALTH

Insurance
Nationals of EU member countries can get medical treatment in state hospitals with the relevant documentation (Form E111 for UK nationals), although private medical insurance is still advised and is essential for all other visitors. Most private clinics and doctors in the Algarve will treat you in your hotel provided you have insurance cover.

Dental Services
Dental services in the Algarve are excellent. Dentists advertise their services in the free English and German-language magazines available from most hotels, and in the monthly publication called *Algarve Living.*

Sun Advice
The sun can be intense in the Algarve at any time of the year, and it is possible to burn with less than an hour's exposure. If you are out walking on cliff-tops or bare hills, it is best to cover vulnerable parts of your body, including your neck, legs and arms.

Drugs
Chemists (*farmâcia*) are open Mon–Fri 9–1 and 3–7, and Sat 9–1. Some open through lunch, and there is a late-night duty rota, posted in pharmacy windows. Take supplies of any drugs that you take regularly, since there is no guarantee that they will be available locally. However, many drugs are available from chemists in Portugal that require prescriptions in other countries. This is partly because pharmacists are skilled paramedics, trained to diagnose a range of problems and sell appropriate medicines.

Safe Water
Tap water is safe to drink, but can be unpleasant to taste because of the minerals it contains. Bottled water is widely available; ask for fizzy water (*água com gás*) or still (*água sem gás*).

CONCESSIONS

Students/Youths Museums have lower rates of admission for students, and entry is free for children. Bring a passport or student card as proof of your age.
Senior Citizens Many senior citizens come to the Algarve for the winter months, attracted by warm weather, a low cost of living and heavily discounted low-season long-stay rates. Ask travel agents specialising in Portugal for details.

CLOTHING SIZES

Portugal	UK	Rest of Europe	USA	
46	36	46	36	Suits
48	38	48	38	
50	40	50	40	
52	42	52	42	
54	44	54	44	
56	46	56	46	
41	7	41	8	Shoes
42	7.5	42	8.5	
43	8.5	43	9.5	
44	9.5	44	10.5	
45	10.5	45	11.5	
46	11	46	12	
37	14.5	37	14.5	Shirts
38	15	38	15	
39/40	15.5	39/40	15.5	
41	16	41	16	
42	16.5	42	16.5	
43	17	43	17	
36	8	34	6	Dresses
38	10	36	8	
40	12	38	10	
42	14	40	12	
44	16	42	14	
46	18	44	16	
38	4.5	38	6	Shoes
38	5	38	6.5	
39	5.5	39	7	
39	6	39	7.5	
40	6.5	40	8	
41	7	41	8.5	

WHEN DEPARTING

- Faro airport is small and does not have expansive shopping facilities.
- You must report to the departure terminal of the airport no later than the check-in time indicated on your ticket.
- You must comply with the import regulations of the country you are travelling to (check before departure).

LANGUAGE

The language of the Algarve is Portuguese, but most hoteliers, shopkeepers and restaurateurs also speak English and German. Portuguese is easy to understand in its written form if you already know a Romance language – such as French, Italian or Spanish. When pronounced, however, it could easily be mistaken for a Slavic language. Two sounds are distinctive to Portuguese: vowels accented with a tilda sound like *owoo* (so bread, *pão,* is pronounced *powoo*) and the s and z, which are pronounced *zsh* (so *notas,* banknotes, is pronounced *notazsh*).

hotel	*hotel/estalagem*	a double room	*quarto de casal*
do you have a room?	*tem um quarto livre?*	a twin room	*quarto com duas camas*
I have a reservation	*tenho um quarto reservado*	with bathroom	*com banho*
		one night	*um noite*
how much per night?	*qual e o preço por noite?*	key	*chave*
		sea view	*vista a mar*
a single room	*um quarto simples*	gents/ladies	*senhores/senhors*

bank	*banco*	pounds/dollars	*libras/dólares*
exchange	*office câmbios*	do you take?	*aceitam?*
post office	*correio*	credit card	*cartão de crédito*
coins	*moedas*	traveller's cheque	*cheque de viagem*
banknotes	*notas*		
receipt	*recibo*	cheque	*cheque*
the change	*troco*	how much?	*quanto custa?*
can you change?	*pode trocar?*		

breakfast	*pequeno almoço*	beer	*cerveja*
lunch	*almoço*	menu	*lista*
dinner	*jantar*	red wine	*vinho tinto*
table	*uma mesa*	white wine	*vinho branco*
starter	*entrada*	water	*água*
main course	*prato principal*	tea	*chá*
dessert	*sobremesa*	coffee (black)	*um bica*
bill	*conta*	coffee (white)	*café con leite*

airport	*aeroporto*	which way to?	*como se vai para?*
bus	*autocarro*	how far?	*a que distância?*
bus station	*estação de autocarro*	where is?	*onde está*
		car	*carro*
bus stop	*paragem*	petrol	*gasolina*
a ticket to	*um bilhete para*	petrol station	*posta de gasolina*
single	*ida*		
return	*ida e volta*		

yes	*sim*	good evening/night	*boa noite*
no	*não*		
please	*por favor*	excuse me	*desculpe*
thank you (male)	*obrigado*	you're welcome	*está bem*
thank you (female)	*obrigada*	not at all	*de nada*
hello	*olá*	how are you?	*como está?*
goodbye	*adeus*	well, thank you	*bem, obrigado (a)*
good morning	*bom dia*	do you speak English?	*fala inglês?*
good afternoon	*bom tarde*		
		I don't understand	*não compreendo*

INDEX

Acknowledgements

The Automobile Association wishes to thank the following photographers and libraries for their assistance in the preparation of this book:

ANDALUCIA SLIDE LIBRARY (M CHAPLOW) 15b, 51b, 54c, 55c, 86b, 91a, 92/116, 122c; **B & E ANDERSON** 37c; **MARY EVANS PICTURE LIBRARY** 11b, 14b; **HULTON GETTY** 11c; **NATURE PHOTOGRAPHERS LTD** 73b (SC Bisserott); **PICTURES COLOUR LIBRARY LTD** 70/1; **www.euro.ecb.int/** 119 (euro notes).

All remaining pictures are held in the Association's own library (**AA PHOTO LIBRARY**) and were taken by **M CHAPLOW**, except the following:

M BIRKITT f/cover a (chapel), 23b, 24b, 42, 59b; **J EDMANSON** 6b, 19b, 21b, 37b, 39b, 39c, 46b, 47, 55b, 60, 74b, 88b; **C JONES** f/cover c (statue), d (pottery), e (golfer), f (fishing boat), b/cover; **A KOUPRIANOFF** 5a, 6a, 7a, 8a, 8/9, 9a, 9c, 10a, 10b, 11a, 12a, 12b, 13a, 14a, 15a, 16a, 17a, 18a, 18b, 19a, 20a, 20b, 21a, 22a, 23a, 24a, 25a, 26a, 32b, 34, 52b, 62, 66b, 89b; **P WILSON** f/cover bottom (tiles), 2.

Dear Essential Traveller

Your comments, opinions and recommendations are very important to us. So please help us to improve our travel guides by taking a few minutes to complete this simple questionnaire.

You do not need a stamp (unless posted outside the UK). If you do not want to cut this page from your guide, then photocopy it or write your answers on a plain sheet of paper.

Send to: **The Editor, AA World Travel Guides, FREEPOST SCE 4598, Basingstoke RG21 4GY.**

Your recommendations...

We always encourage readers' recommendations for restaurants, nightlife or shopping – if your recommendation is used in the next edition of the guide, we will send you a ***FREE* AA *Essential* Guide** of your choice. Please state below the establishment name, location and your reasons for recommending it.

____

____

____

____

Please send me **AA *Essential*** ________________________

(see list of titles inside the front cover)

About this guide...

Which title did you buy?

AA *Essential* ____________________________

Where did you buy it? ____________________________

When? m m / y y

Why did you choose an AA *Essential* Guide? ____________________

____

____

____

____

Did this guide meet your expectations?

Exceeded ☐ Met all ☐ Met most ☐ Fell below ☐

Please give your reasons ____________________________

____

____

____

continued on next page...

Were there any aspects of this guide that you particularly liked? ________

____

____

____

Is there anything we could have done better? ________

____

____

____

____

About you...

Name (*Mr/Mrs/Ms*) ________

Address ________

____

________ Postcode ________

Daytime tel nos ________

Which age group are you in?

Under 25 ☐ 25–34 ☐ 35–44 ☐ 45–54 ☐ 55–64 ☐ 65+ ☐

How many trips do you make a year?

Less than one ☐ One ☐ Two ☐ Three or more ☐

Are you an AA member? Yes ☐ No ☐

About your trip...

When did you book? m m / y y When did you travel? m m / y y

How long did you stay? ________

Was it for business or leisure? ________

Did you buy any other travel guides for your trip?

If yes, which ones? ________

____

Thank you for taking the time to complete this questionnaire. Please send it to us as soon as possible, and remember, you do not need a stamp (*unless posted outside the UK*).

Happy Holidays!